Grace I Never Knew

by Terry M. Southers

Written in memory of

Kristy Nicole (Southers) Woodcox
December 6, 1977 - May 8, 2005

Danielle (Dani) Faith Woodcox
September 22, 2001 - May 1, 2005

Written in dedication to my grandchildren

Gabriel Matthias
Terryann Nicole
Aaryn Paige

Table of Contents

Acknowledgments

I must express a special "thank you" to those who have supported me and made the writing of this book possible.

My Lord and Savior, Jesus Christ, who carried me when I was unable to walk.

My wife, Stephanie, who is not just my wife and help mate but is also my best friend. Thank you for your sacrifice and endurance through all the hours it took in writing "Grace I Never Knew."

Jim and Helen Southers, my father and mother who have always been a great source of strength and encouragement to me. Thank you for teaching me the ways and truths of God. You have never failed to be there when I needed you the most.

Jim and Paula Fraley, who made themselves available to us at any hour of the day. Thank you for laughing with us, crying with us, praying with us and allowing us to share our hearts as you patiently listened. Thank you for those weekend trips to the Amish country that always came at just the right time.

Clay Burgett, my good friend and brother in Christ. Thank you for sacrificing time from your busy schedule to edit this book. You, **Patti**, and your three boys will always hold a special place in my and Steph's heart.

The Heritage Free Will Baptist Church, whose love, support and sacrifice toward us have been unending. It is truly my and Stephanie's honor and privilege to call you our brothers and sisters in Christ. The only thing that can be better than worshipping with you on this earth is to know that we will live with you throughout eternity in heaven.

A Word from Terry

B efore you actually start reading "Grace I Never Knew" I would like to share with you what inspired me to write it. First and foremost, I want to bring glory to Jesus Christ. He is deserving of all the praise and honor that we bestow upon Him. If we will allow Him, He will teach us how to praise Him in the bad times, as well as the good. I pray that this book will give Him the glory that He is worthy of.

I do have a few other reasons for writing this book. I want to keep the memories of my daughter and grand-daughter alive. Those who personally knew Kristy and Dani will testify of how they touched the lives of everyone with whom they came in contact. So many others have said to me, "I wish I would have had the opportunity to know them better than I did." I wrote a chapter on each one of their lives to secure their memory and to allow others to know exactly how special they really were.

Several chapters are especially written for Kristy's three children who she left behind. At the time of the accident Gabriel was six-years old, Terryann was five and Aaryn Paige was only eight-months old. Gabe and Terryann still talk about their mom, but I fear that in time their memories may fade. The chapters about their mommy and sister are something they will always have to hold on to as they get older. Memories may fade, but I want them to always know how special their mother was and how much she loved them. Aaryn has no memory of her mother whatsoever, so I wanted to provide her with something that she could cherish in later years. I want her to know who awaits her in heaven.

The later chapters deal with the accident, the adjustments of moving on and the amazing grace of our Heavenly Father. Anytime my wife and I hear of someone losing a loved one, especially a child, our hearts become burdened for that individual. We have experienced that pain and we hurt with them. By sharing our story we hope to offer hope to those experiencing similar heartaches. We want you to know that God has not left you, even though you may feel as such. His grace is more than able to get you through, and He has an abundant supply.

As you read "Grace I Never Knew," you will realize this book is meant to do nothing more than give praise to the One who sustained me during my weakest moments. I exalt the Lord Jesus Christ who never gave up on me when I almost gave up on myself. Without God, I cannot begin to help anyone through the trial or hardship that they may be experiencing. I can tell you what He did for me, though. My prayer is that, as others read about how my wife and I have felt His healing touch, this book will help them in their time of need. Truly, if you have a need, He has the answer.

In Christ,

Terry M. Southers
terry.southers@yahoo.com

Introduction

*My grace is sufficient for thee: for my strength is
made perfect in weakness.*
(1 Corinthians 12:9)

The apostle Paul talked about a thorn in the flesh, something which was troubling to him. It was Paul's desire
for the Lord to remove this thorn. We cannot be certain what
the thorn was that troubled Brother Paul, but there is little
doubt that this great man of God felt that he could be more
beneficial to the Lord if it were removed from him. God
thought different though. *My thoughts are not your thoughts,
neither are my ways your ways, saith the Lord (Isaiah 55:8).*
In a way that only God knows, He knew that Paul's trials
would ultimately be for his own good, and those same trials
would work to Paul's advantage in his work for the Lord.
The trials and afflictions that Paul would suffer would bring
glory to God. Though his trials may not have been easy to
bear and they were not what Paul desired, God knew that
the grace He provided would be sufficient to get His servant
through anything that he may face during his ministry and
lifetime. The same God that provided the necessary grace to
carry this great apostle through his trials is the same God that
provides the necessary grace to sustain us as well. Through
his struggles and hardships Paul learned to trust in God. It

was during those times that He learned that the promises of God are true. *I will never leave thee, nor forsake thee (Hebrews 13:5)* was a promise that Paul learned well. God's amazing grace abided continually with this great apostle, and every obstacle overcome only made his faith grow stronger in the One who was so real to him. Paul learned to be content regardless of what he faced in this life (Philippians 4:11). His God never failed him. He knew that whatever he needed would be provided by His Lord.

My Grandma Southers had many hardships and endured many tragedies in her lifetime. She had nine children precede her in death, ranging from the ages of a few months, to thirty-eight. Her husband died in June 1964, and one week later her son was killed right in front of her own house. Many people questioned how one person was able to cope with so many tragedies in her lifetime. She was able to cope because of God's grace. God supplied my grandmother with grace that many people have never known or understood. God doesn't give this kind of grace to everyone. Not everyone needs it. His grace is endless, but it is also given only as needed. Grace is something that only God can give, and its purpose is to help us through our present problem. The greatest and most necessary kind of grace is God's saving grace. You, me, and everyone else who will be born, still living, or has already died, were born into sin. God's penalty for sin is death. Through His saving grace, God allowed His Son, Jesus Christ, our Savior, to take our place by giving His own life when He willingly died on Calvary's cross. Everyone is in need of saving grace, but not everyone needs the kind of grace it takes to overcome the loss of a child or loved one.

Let me try to illustrate further what I mean. You wouldn't give crutches to someone who had two perfectly good legs. Why not? Because they wouldn't need them. They are able to walk on their own. They don't need crutches to help them through their problem. Those crutches sure come in handy for the person who has a broken leg, though. That's the way God's grace is. Grace is given only when necessary, and only God knows what kind of grace is needed for each situation.

Why can't we fully grasp or understand all there is to know about God in this life? It is because His love, mercy, and grace are too far-reaching; so much more than the human, finite mind can even begin to comprehend or understand.

God's grace covers every circumstance, obstacle, problem, or sin that man can ever come in contact with. His grace covers anything that each individual He ever created may need during their particular lifetime; grace that will see them through all of life's trials, temptations, struggles and battles.

We must realize that each person needs God's grace extended to them in a way that is unique; in a way that only He can do. For this reason it is impossible to understand that part of God's grace which supplies or sustains an individual at their needed time or moment. In turn, it's impossible for you to understand the grace which carries me through my most needed moment.

God made each one of us different, and each one is unique in our Heavenly Father's eyes. Therefore each person will face different tests and trials during their lifetime on this earth. Every test, trial, temptation, or obstacle which we face requires our Heavenly Father's grace to sustain us, and each time we come through those difficult times we will gain a better understanding of our omniscient, omnipotent and omnipresent, yet reachable, God. Unless a person were exposed to every test, trial, temptation, obstacle, problem or sin that was ever known to mankind since the beginning of creation, it would be impossible for them to know God in His entirety.

Yes, right now we do see through a glass darkly. We only see and comprehend what we personally need for us as individuals, which will allow us to live by faith. Thank God though, one glorious day, we will see and understand Him in His fullness. Until then, we must learn to love and appreciate what we do know and understand, not question what we don't know and don't understand. Only then will we be able to experience the peace, joy, and contentment of serving God which He intends for us to know in this life.

Chapter 1

My Testimony

Therefore if any man be in Christ, he is a new crea-
ture: old things are passed away;
behold, all things are become new.
(2 Corinthians 5:17)

Every Christian should have a testimony. I'm talking about being able to pinpoint a particular time or date that their life was transformed through their salvation experience. For me, that date was January 22, 1978. As a matter of fact, my wife Stephanie and I both gave our hearts to the Lord on that same night. We had been married for about a year and a half, and our baby daughter, Kristy Nicole was seven weeks old. I will never forget that night. It was a cold and wintry evening as we knelt down at an old fashioned altar in a little brick church and asked Jesus Christ into our hearts. I can honestly say that my life has never been the same since. Though I have failed my Lord many times over the years, I can truthfully say that He has never failed me even once.

I was raised in a Christian home so I understood at a young age what it meant to be saved. My heart goes out to

Grace I Never Knew

anyone who wasn't raised in church nor has no concept of salvation as taught by the Bible. That's why it's so important that we reach our children at a young and tender age. Someone once told me that if you can talk to a child about God at the age of ten, there is better than a ninety percent chance that he or she will accept Jesus Christ. They went on to say that if you talk to an unsaved person at age ninety, there is less than a ten percent chance that they will even listen to you. I believe there is much truth to that statement.

Though I knew about God and His plan of salvation as a child, I didn't get saved until the age of twenty-one. I had rejected God my whole life. This is what I want you to understand. I want you to see the amazing love of a Heavenly Father who is not demanding, but He is gentle, caring and kind; and He is continually knocking at your heart's door, asking for permission to live in your heart. God is patient when working with the one He is calling out. He desires your fellowship and He is offering you the greatest gift you could ever receive. He is offering you eternal life in heaven.

If the Lord is dealing with your heart right now, it's important that you don't put Him off. Don't live with the attitude that "I will do it later". That is so dangerous. If you wake up one morning and discover that you don't feel the same convictions that you did before then I have to warn you. You are the one that moved, not God. It's possible to reject God for so long that your heart can become callous to His touch and deaf to His call. I have often feared that, had I not accepted the Lord when I did, my heart may have become callous to the convicting of the Holy Spirit, even to the point of not being able to sense His wooing as He knocked at my heart's door.

I can remember as a child, no more than seven or eight years of age, how the Lord would talk with me. I didn't understand then what I do now. Back then I thought I was just fearing the thought of dying and going to hell. I later understood though that it was actually God speaking to my heart at a very young age. I can remember lying in bed at night, knowing that I needed a change in my life, and I knew that unless I accepted Jesus Christ as my Lord and Savior I risked spending eternity in a hell that was prepared for the devil and his angels.

Some may be tempted to say, "How much wrong could you have done at such a young age that you would have inherited hell as your eternal home if you had died?" This is an important truth that needs to be understood by every unsaved person. Each one of us is born into a world of sin. We are all born sinners, and we are in need of a Savior to rescue us from the penalty of that sin, which is eternal death. Jesus Christ paid the penalty for us with His death on the cross.

That would lead to another question which is often asked, "At what age does a person become accountable for their wrongdoing?" The answer is when you know right from wrong. This is so hard for many people because most believe that they haven't really done anything wrong, at least nothing bad enough to merit the punishment of hell. The Bible makes it clear that even one wrongdoing is sin, and all sin must be accounted for in God's eyes. Our Heavenly Father is a Holy God, who is without sin. No sin can enter into heaven. No sin or wrongdoing, regardless of how small it may seem in your eyes, will go unpunished. Therefore, all of us are without hope of ever entering heaven unless our sin problem is solved. Jesus Christ is our problem solver. God's payment for the penalty of sin is death. Jesus died on the cross for you and me and for all of mankind. Romans 5:8 says, "...*God commendeth his love toward us, in that, while we were yet sinners, Christ died for us.*" The blood that He shed that day appeased the wrath of God. There is your answer my friend. You can do nothing to please God within yourself. Your sins must be dealt with. Since Jesus did it for you, you must go to Him, admit that you are a sinner and ask forgiveness for your sins, and He will do just that. You are now saved and on your way to heaven. Sounds too easy, doesn't it? That is the Scriptural way though, plain and simple.

Steph and I get married on September 4, 1976. I was twenty and she just turned eighteen. By now I had pushed God so far to the back burner that I was like one of those people who said, "I will get saved, but not right now." I had grown cold in my heart and was ignoring the pleas of the Lord to accept Him as my Savior. God never gave up on me.

In April 1977, Steph found out she was pregnant. It was during those months of her pregnancy that the Lord started convicting me like I had never experienced before. I was one miserable person as I was trying to live one way, while at the same time, God was asking for me to give my life to Him. If you have ever experienced the convicting power of God, you know exactly what I am talking about. I believe it to be worse than any physical illness that I've ever encountered.

During those months of waiting for Steph to give birth to our new baby I did a lot of soul searching. I started thinking about how I was responsible for bringing my children up to know God. God used the birth of my child to once again get my attention. I knew the truth, and even though I was gambling with my own salvation, was I going to deny my child the opportunity to know the truth about God, Satan, heaven and hell?

I started making deals and promises with God. When my baby was born, then I would consider getting right and going to church. What a wonderful God we serve that He would even be willing to listen to our helpless and often empty and broken promises. It helped for a while as I convinced myself that God was now happy with me. At least I was now acknowledging His rightful presence in my life. God must have felt real honored. Yeah, right!

I wanted a boy, hands down. A girl was out of the question. In 1977 it wasn't that common for the husband to be in the delivery room with the expectant mother, and believe me, I wanted no part of it. On December 6, 1977, at 7:07 pm, Kristy Nicole Southers was born to Terry and Stephanie Southers at Mount Carmel West Hospital in Columbus, Ohio. I later discovered that when Steph found out we had a girl she started crying because she thought I would be upset. Let me tell you what was going on in that waiting room though.

Yes, I did want a boy. I wanted a boy really bad. But then about that last hour or so before Kristy was born I started getting real scared. I started thinking about all the things that could go wrong. My heart was about to beat out of my chest and I started praying. As sincerely as I knew how I again made another deal with God. I prayed, "Oh God, please let Steph and my baby be all right. Let the baby just be healthy, God. And Lord, I don't care if it's a boy or a girl, just let everything be all right." Of course I didn't end my prayer before promising God that if He would just answer this prayer I would start going to church. Be careful what you promise God. He doesn't forget, nor will He let you forget.

I remember standing behind that glass picture window looking at all those newborn babies. I saw the nurse pick Kristy up. She counted her fingers and toes and checked over every part of her little body. Then she brought her over to the window for me to look at her. Let me tell you, I was one proud daddy. I stood there with tears in my eyes. Already, Kristy was daddy's girl. I had totally forgotten all that stuff about wanting a boy. God had been so good to me. I told Him thank you right then and there.

21

I went to work the next day and started passing out cigars to everyone. "It's a Girl," the wrapper said, and I couldn't have been prouder. I even gave a cigar to one of the Christian men I worked with. I told him, "I know you don't smoke, but keep it as a souvenir." Bob smiled and took the cigar, and I continued making my rounds.

The next day Bob came to me and gave the cigar back. He said, "Terry, I don't want to offend you but I just can't keep this cigar. You see, I don't smoke and I don't believe God would be pleased with me keeping it. I hope you understand." What Bob didn't realize was that not only did I understand, but I respected him for living by his convictions. That act of faithfulness to the God he served spoke volumes to me. Up to that time Bob and I were just co-workers, but God was about to use him in a great way to witness to me.

Over the next week or so I really started feeling the convicting power of the Holy Spirit working in my life. God would not let me forget the promises that I made to Him. I couldn't sleep well at night and I was an absolute wreck inside. I was at an all-time high for feeling miserable, knowing that I needed the Lord in my life, and I was close to giving in. Then the devil got involved in the picture. He knew I was seeking answers and he tried his best to get in the way.

I started sitting with Bob during lunch and at break times. I remember him saying to me, "Terry, God has his hand on you and I know He is speaking to your heart. I'd like to invite you to church with me." I was so close, but then my working buddies started riding me, and they wouldn't let up. They would make comments like, "Hey man, are you turning religious on us? You sure are spending a lot of time with Bob." They would laugh; then I would laugh. I couldn't take their scoffing and criticism though. Over the next few days I quit hanging around Bob. I knew he realized what was going on, but he never did force the issue. He just kept praying for me.

God will go to any length to reach a lost soul. I am living proof of that. It was obvious that I was ashamed to be made fun of for the sake of Jesus Christ. I didn't even want to be seen talking to Bob at work anymore. God had every right to simply turn away from me. After all, if I was ashamed of Him, why should He want me? He never gave up on me though.

By now I was crumbling inside. Something had to give. The conviction of the Holy Spirit warring against the onslaught of the devil was about to tear me apart, both physically and mentally. I needed to talk to Bob but just couldn't handle the peer pressure. I want you to see how much my Heavenly Father loved me.

I prayed and asked the Lord to provide a way for me to talk with Bob without anyone knowing it. I even explained to God that I just didn't have the courage to stand against my buddies at work. I needed His help. I've often heard that God doesn't hear the prayers of the unsaved. I know He does hear and He will respond when that unsaved individual has become broken inside and has nowhere else to turn. I wasn't saved yet, but He was speaking to me nonetheless. If He was speaking to me, then I have to believe that He was listening to me as well.

There was a special project about to get started in my department at work. This project would require two people working together for the next several days in an area of the plant where they would be alone. Can you guess who they chose for this job? Bob and I were selected. I couldn't believe it. Even with all of my sin, constant failures, and the lack of courage to stand up for God, He still answered my prayers. This touched me more than words could ever say.

Bob and I worked side-by-side over the next several days. I am not exaggerating when I say that we would spend the entire shift talking about God. The job we were assigned to allowed for us to have conversation even while we worked. It was absolutely amazing. God knew just what I needed, and He provided the answer. That time alone with my new friend transformed my life. I had not yet given my life to Christ, but I was a changed person, nonetheless. By this time I was ignoring the comments by the other workers. I was ready to take the next step. I told Bob that I wanted to go to church with Him.

Steph knew something was going on with me. She was not only supportive, but she recognized her need for God as well. We made arrangements to go to church that following Sunday morning, January 22, 1978. I couldn't wait!

I want to make something clear right here. A person doesn't have to be saved in a church. I was more than ready, and I could have been saved even before stepping foot in that church building. You see, it's the position of one's heart that saves them, not the position of his or her body. In other words, you don't have to physically kneel at an altar in order to be saved. For me personally, I just felt the need to go up to an altar in a church and give my heart to Jesus. God graciously provided me that opportunity.

Sunday morning came. I'll be honest with you. I didn't hear much of what was said, sung, or preached in that service. I could only feel the tug of the Lord at my heart's door, pleading with me to get out of my seat and make my way up to that altar. Guess what? I didn't go. I just sat there. I got so scared that I couldn't move. The devil hadn't given up yet either.

Bob and his wife Sandy invited Steph and me to spend that afternoon with them. We had a wonderful dinner and sat around and just talked until it was time to go back to the evening service. Bob never mentioned anything about me not going up to pray that morning. He knew what was going on inside of me and he was confident that God would win!

The evening service was almost a carbon copy of that morning. I sat there hearing nothing, because I knew what I needed to do. During the altar call it was like I was frozen in my seat. I knew that I could not leave that building that night without getting things right between God and myself. I remember someone saying one time that if you would take the first step God would take you the rest of the way. I was about to find out if that was true or not.

I stood up, stepped out into the aisle, and took one step, and what I had heard was true. I couldn't get to that altar quick enough. As I was walking it seemed as if years of burdens were falling off of me with each step. Remember, it's not the position of the body, but rather the position of the heart. As soon as I determined in my heart to go forward, I believe that I was saved. I'm not saying that everyone's salvation experience has to be like mine. Please don't think that is what I am implying. I can only testify of what happened to me.

Tears were streaming down my face even before I knelt at that altar. People may wonder why someone would cry when they get saved. I can tell you why. For the first time in my entire life I knew how it felt to be free. Years of guilt, sin, and shame fell from me like water rolling down a hillside. I can't praise my Savior enough for what He did for me that night! If you have never experienced this, it cannot be put into words that give its meaning justice. I can only relate it to what the blind man said whom Jesus touched and healed, *"One thing I know, that, whereas I was blind, now I see"* (John 9:25).

My evening was made complete when I later discovered that Steph came forward, too! God had never given up on me! He patiently waited for me. How loving He is. Because of Him I now have eternal life in Christ Jesus. Steph, Kristy, and I were about to start our new lives living for God. My little girl was going to grow up in the ways of the Lord. I could not have been happier!

I wondered all night what I would say to the guys at work. I was a new person in Christ Jesus, and I now had the courage to stand up for my convictions. I just wanted to make sure that I gave my God all the glory. As it turned out, I didn't have to say anything. It was as if they knew something had happened to me. Of course, I did take every opportunity to tell them what Jesus did for me, but they didn't act as they did before. They didn't make fun, scoff, laugh, or anything. For the most part, at first they just shied away from me. I don't think they could believe that I really did get saved. I didn't want my commitment to Christ to just be words, though. I wanted my life to show it. I have failed the Lord many times since my conversion, but I have always tried to be sincere with my walk before an unbelieving world.

I hope in some way my testimony spoke to your heart. If you are already saved, maybe my testimony will strengthen you in some way. If you aren't saved, my prayer is that it will speak to your heart. I am no exception to God's love, mercy, and grace. What he did for me, He wants to do for you as well. I only hope and pray that you will make that decision to accept Him before it is too late (God's plan for salvation is included at the end of this book). Jesus said in Revelation 3:20, *"Behold, I stand at the door and knock: if any man hear my voice, and open the door, I will come in to him, and will sup with him, and he with me."* Won't you invite Him in today?

Chapter 2

"Kristy"

Who can find a virtuous woman? For her price is
far above rubies.
(Proverbs 31:10)

When the Bible speaks of a virtuous woman as in Proverbs 31:10, it is talking about a woman of character, a woman of strength, a woman who desires to please God in all that she says and does. Kristy's ambition in this life was to be all that God wanted her to be. I believe that Kristy was a virtuous woman as described in Proverbs, and her price was far above rubies.

Many people have said to me since her death, "I always admired the way Kristy was such a good mother to her four children. You could just see how much she loved and cared for each one of them. I wish I had known her better."

Those who knew Kristy will testify to the kind of mother and person she was. This chapter is written to tell about her life.

I especially wrote this chapter for my grandchildren; Gabriel, Terryann, and Aaryn Paige. They were so young when their mommy died that I wanted to give them something they could treasure forever. This book is a way that they can keep her memory alive. Aaryn was only eight-months when the accident happened, so she undoubtedly has no recollection of her mother, whatsoever. I am so glad that we have the home videos showing Kristy with her children. I want them to know how much she loved them. We have recordings of her singing during church services, as well as her testimony, so they will know how much serving God was such an integral part of her life.

Kristy loved everyone, and her death hit our church family really hard, especially so many of the young women with whom she was such good friends. Many of them were kind enough to write a letter to Aaryn about how special Kristy was. Those letters are stored, and when the time is right, we will give them to Aaryn. I'm sure they will be a priceless treasure to her.

I will briefly touch on Kristy's childhood, but I want to devote the majority of the chapter to her life as an adult. Her adulthood was the time in her life when she most notably touched the lives of those who mattered the most to her: her children.

We can look at each one of our grandkids and see Kristy. Each one of them shows a different resemblance or trait which assures us that our daughter will always be remembered through their individual lives alone.

Dani had more of Kristy's natural qualities than any of the other kids. She had the same blond hair, the same blue eyes, and even the same smile that Kristy wore as a baby, but each one of them was loved equally by their mommy.

Kristy developed a love for God at an early age. She was about the age of seven or eight when she asked Jesus into her heart. She was a special child who had convictions even at that young age. No one will ever be able to convince me that a child at that age is too young to understand what they are doing. Gabriel was five years of age when he made his decision to accept Jesus, and Terryann was six. They both often talk about how they know that one day they will see their mommy and little sister again. There is nothing quite like the faith of a child.

So often new Christians will stumble along the way, and sometimes they may even fall out of church. I hate to admit it, but I was no exception. The year was 1983, and the church that Steph and I got saved in was going through some internal struggles and issues. There ended up being a church split, and it actually became a very ugly mess. We were terribly hurt over some of the things which transpired, and as a result we left the church.

When I left that church I had every intention of finding another church. I thought I just needed to take a break for a while, though. That break lasted almost three years. It was a huge mistake not to find another church right away. I had allowed my hurt to turn bitter, and it wasn't long before I lost my desire to go to church altogether. I was now on a backslidden path that would take me down some very rough terrain as the Lord chastised me until I came back to Him. Please let this be a lesson to you. There is no good reason to stop attending church. Christians need to understand the necessity of attending and being committed to their local church. God uses the church and the body of believers in that church to exhort, encourage, and carry one another's burdens (just to name a few of the many benefits of this command-ment of our Lord (Hebrews 10:25)).

The church is where we hear God's Word taught and preached, which in turn feeds and nourishes our spirit. Many will argue that one doesn't have to go to church to be saved, but I wholeheartedly believe that without the continual fellow-ship of our brothers and sisters in a Bible preaching church, we are dangerously treading on waters that may easily lead us to compromise and to a backslidden condition.

Kristy was very instrumental to my faith during that time in my life. Steph and Kristy wanted to go to church again. Steph worked with a man who attended the North Free Will Baptist Church in Columbus, OH. He invited her to his church, and she and Kristy went. I told her that was fine but not to expect me to go. I was a miserable person at that time, and I wouldn't allow myself the opportunity to receive the healing that I so desperately needed. I was trying to convince myself that I was all right. After all, I wasn't as bad as I used to be. The bottom line though is that I was out of fellowship with my Savior, and He would not let me forget it. Thank God for the convicting power of the Holy Spirit. What a God we serve that will never give up on us, even when we have given up on ourselves!

There was one particular Sunday I will never forget. Steph and Kristy were getting ready to leave for the evening service. Kristy came up to me and said, "Daddy, won't you please come with us?" I told her no. I don't think I ever felt worse than I did at that moment. My convictions were pouncing hard upon me. I should have been the spiritual head of my home. I should have been the one leading my family out the door to church, but it was my eight-year-old daughter trying to get me back in church. That evening was the start of my restitution with the Lord Jesus Christ. I owe it all to a faithful wife and my persistent eight-year-old daughter.

I started going to church with my family again. Kristy loved to sing, and she was already starting to get involved in the ministry that would continue through her adulthood. Even at that young age she sang from her heart and her sincerity was plain to see. I was so proud of her as she would stand at the front of the church and sing with all of her heart unto the

Lord. More importantly though, I know that her Heavenly Father was even more pleased than I was.

I know this is coming from a prejudiced father, but I am as honest as I can be when I say that during her teen years, my daughter was as close to being the perfect child as one could get. Am I saying that she never erred or never made mistakes? No, in that sense we know that no one is perfect. That's the reason Jesus had to come and die for each one of us. His death paid the price for our sins, shortcomings, and failures that we in ourselves could do nothing about.

Kristy never gave her mother or me one problem in all of the years we raised her. She would come home from school, and it was just automatic that she would do her homework. We never had to tell her to do so; she just did it. We never had to fight with her to get ready for school. Even in her elementary years she would get ready for school as soon as we called for her to wake up. It was very rare that she ever missed a day of school. If she did you knew that she was sick. I can remember days that I would try to get her to stay home, because I thought she wasn't feeling well, but she insisted that she was all right and would go anyway. She always was a very responsible child, and this, too, carried on throughout her teenage years and into her adult, married life as well.

I do have to tell about one incident though that will stay with us forever. It was a Friday night, and Kristy and three girls from her youth group spent the night together at the house of one of the girls. Kristy was either sixteen or seventeen at the time. Because she had proven herself to act so responsibly, we let her drive over to her friend's house.

I worked third shift at that time, and at about two o'clock that morning I received a phone call from Steph. With the slightest twist of irony in her voice she said to me, "Do you know where I am right now?" From her vocal expression I could tell that the answer to that loaded question was not one that I would have even been able to dream up. "No," I said. "At 2:00 o'clock in the morning, I would hope your answer would be, 'home,' but somehow I just don't think that's what you're going to tell me." Steph went on to say that she was at the Grove City police station where our daughter and her three friends were being held for being out after curfew.

Steph went on to explain how Kristy and her friends decided it would be fun to slip out of the house after everyone was in bed. Then they would go toilet paper the house of someone they knew. Their little plan got nixed when a police officer drove by and shined his spotlight on them. They took off running and tried to hide in a nearby field. Every one of those girls had chigger bites all over them. It only got worse for Kristy though. She was the driver of this gang of desperados, and the police now had her car in custody. She had to come forward. Keep in mind now, we are talking about someone who had never been in an ounce of trouble a day in her entire life. She was now seeing her life pass before her. She only hoped and prayed they wouldn't use tear gas or start shooting! In the wisdom of her youth she thought it might be best to peaceably surrender, and maybe she would get out early for good behavior!

As for Steph, she couldn't believe the events that had just taken place, and I couldn't believe what I was hearing. While still talking to Steph, I said, "Kristy, our Kristy, caught toilet papering a house at two o'clock in the morning!" I'm telling you the truth, you could have lined up every kid in that church from the youngest to the oldest, and Kristy would have been the last one I would have picked to be a part of this! After the initial shock of it all, we had to laugh. Anyone but Kristy!

Eventually, all of the other parents started showing up at the police station. One of the other mothers walked up to Steph and said, "What are you doing here?" Steph replied, "I'm here for the same reason you are. Our daughters were in this together." Almost in disbelief the mother said, "Kristy? I have no problem believing my daughter would do this, but Kristy?" Over the years we occasionally run into one of those girls or one of their mothers, and we still laugh about it. Kristy would laugh about it, too. She always said, "The only time in my life I did something I knew I shouldn't have, and I got caught. Can you believe it? It just doesn't seem fair." That's the way Kristy was. She loved having a good time. She liked to joke and laugh. One of her great qualities was her ability to laugh at herself.

Kristy was very smart in school and she excelled in everything she took part in. She easily had the intelligence to further her education in about any field she so desired. In the tenth grade she decided that she wanted a career in cosmetology. I tried to talk her out of it. I wanted her to go on to college, but at the same time I respected her judgment to make her own decisions. So, in her junior year she enrolled at the Fairfield Career Center. She spent the next two years learning the art of cosmetology. She became very skilled at her profession too, I might add. That was no great surprise to any one who knew her, though. Whatever she did, she put her whole heart into it.

The career center proved to be a very valuable experience for Kristy. She became involved in the VICA (Vocational Industrial Clubs of America) program. Kristy's cosmetology teacher, Janet Miller, was one of the adult leaders in VICA. Janet and Kristy became more than teacher and student. They became very good friends, and Janet recognized Kristy's potential and ability to attain higher levels.

Janet encouraged Kristy to run for one of the offices in VICA. Everyone liked Kristy, and she easily won the position of National Secretary. Steph and I had reservations because we knew this position would take our daughter away from home from time to time. We met with Janet, and she persuaded us to believe that she only had Kristy's best interest at heart. We also became close to Janet during those years, and we learned to trust her to watch over our daughter while she was away from home. Even after Kristy graduated she kept in contact with her mentor/teacher. Janet was absolutely heartbroken when she learned of Kristy's untimely death. She told Steph and me that in all of her years of teaching she never had or met any student like Kristy. She told us how Kristy touched her life and she will be remembered in her heart forever.

Kristy's position as National Secretary made her the student spokesperson for VICA. Her responsibilities took her all over the country as a guest speaker. Her travels took her to Washington DC, Kansas City, and San Francisco, where she spoke to literally thousands of people on behalf of VICA. Steph and I were invited as guests when she spoke to an audience of five thousand people at the Aladdin Shrine Temple in Columbus, OH. She received a standing ovation, and I know that her mother and I were beaming brighter than the lights that were focused upon her.

Throughout this time, Kristy never lost her Christian morals and values. One of her speeches included using the Bible as a reference. One of the promotional directors told her that referencing the Bible might not be a good idea and to leave that part out of her speech. Kristy would not budge. She asked me what she should do. I told her to live by her convictions. That is exactly what she did. Kristy told them that the speech stayed the way she wrote it or someone else would have to give it. Guess what? The speech stayed the same.

Kristy was a remarkable student. Along with all of her VICA awards, her most amazing accomplishment came from her home school, Teays Valley, where she attended her first two years of high school. She made the National Honor

Society at Teays Valley and at the Fairfield Career Center as well. Achieving both was a very rare accomplishment.

Again, Kristy had the ability to become just about anything she wanted to become. However, by her senior year she knew exactly what she wanted out of life. Her desire was to be a wife and a mother. She always said that she wanted a big family. She knew her mom and dad would have gladly paid for the furtherance of her education, but she insisted on waiting upon the Lord to see what plans He may have for her life.

Kristy graduated from high school in May 1996. In July of that year she met Matthew Woodcox, her future husband. She and Matt married on March 8, 1997. Her life was starting to be all that she had hoped and prayed for. She wanted to be a wife and a mother. On June 26, 1998, she gave birth to Gabriel Matthias. She then followed with three girls. Terryann Nicole was born December 1, 1999, Danielle Faith arrived on September 22, 2001, and Aaryn Paige completed the family on September 3, 2004. Having a large family at a young age may have seemed like a burden to many, but it was an absolute joy to Kristy. She loved her children more than life itself. We often teased her that she was trying to make up for the fact that she was an only child!

As a matter of fact Kristy loved all children. She was very active in the children's ministries at the church. She once told me that she could never have a home church that has no vision for children. Her heart ached every time she met a child whose home life appeared to have problems. She always tried to give extra attention to those children. I believe this made her appreciate and love her own children all the more.

Kristy had a very active wit and sense of humor. She loved people, and she loved to have fun. She enjoyed laughter and was always willing to be in on a good joke. I will never forget hearing her laugh. When her kids would do something funny she would get so tickled that she could hardly talk. She would try to stop long enough to say to me, "Go get the camcorder, this is hilarious."

I remember one time she pulled a prank on Matt. It was after dark, and he had to go out to the garage to get something. You have to get this picture in your mind, now: their garage was unattached to the house, and it was about thirty feet from the back door. Matt only wore boxers as he headed to his destination. As soon as he started back to the house, Kristy flipped on the outside light. There stood Matt in nothing but his boxers in clear view of the neighbors on both sides. Taken by surprise, he froze in his tracks like a deer in the headlights. Kristy flipped the lights off for a second, then back on. She continued this little charade, all the while Matt stopping and starting, not sure whether to run for the house or scurry back to the garage. I believe it was as funny hearing her tell it as the actual joke was itself. I'm not sure Matt saw the humor, but it was something he got used to being married to Kristy. A remarkable thing about Kristy was her ability to laugh when the joke was on her as well. If you did pull one on her you had better beware, though, because she would get you back!

Kristy loved fellowshipping, especially with the other young couples in the church. She was always ready to get together with other people. Right before she died she was in the middle of organizing a fellowship night at the church with my Sunday School class. I could always count on her to help with such things, and she was more than willing to do it. After she died, I just couldn't continue to put the fellowship event together. A couple of the young women in my class stepped forward and made it happen. I was so grateful to them, and I know that Kristy would have been pleased.

As I mentioned, Kristy loved being with the other young couples in the church. It didn't matter if it was a large group, dinner at another couple's house, or dinner at her own house. She was a friend to all of the young women, and it really used to bother her when two of them were not getting along about something. She was a friend to everyone, and she never wanted to take sides. She was a good listener too. All of the young women were affected greatly by Kristy's death, and more than one of them shared with Steph how Kristy was the one person they knew they could always count on. Tears still well up in their eyes when they talk about Kristy. She will always be greatly missed.

When I think of Kristy as a daughter, I guess the first thing that comes to mind is Exodus 20:12: God's fifth commandment, which is to honor thy father and thy mother. Kristy always honored her mother and me from the time she was a little girl until she reached adulthood.

Kristy really was an extraordinary daughter. How many kids do you know that would have wanted their mom and dad living right next to them when they left home? Matt and Kristy had only been married for a couple of years when they bought a home in Grove City, OH. A year later the house two doors from them became vacant, and Kristy begged her mom and me to buy it. She wanted us to be close to her and the kids.

Even after she was married it wasn't uncommon for her to call her mother or me while we were at work just to say that she was thinking about us. There were many times that she would call to say, "I was just thinking about you. I don't want or need anything. I just want you to know that I love you." Do you have any idea what that does to a mom or dad? There was nothing I wouldn't have done for her. I have often used her as an illustration about how pleased our Heavenly Father would be if we would approach Him the same way.

"I don't want anything Father. I just want to say that 'I love you'." If you want to move the heart of God, then pray that way. I guarantee that it makes Him want to bless you beyond measure.

Kristy loved to talk about the Bible. I used to pick up Gabe and Terryann for school. I would drop them off, come back to her house, and we would sit and talk for hours about something in God's Word. She always had a question about one thing or another and wanted to know what I thought about it. She was very studious in God's Word and had a desire to grow in His grace and knowledge.

I announced my calling into the ministry on July 27, 2004, at the age of forty-eight. You want to talk about scared. Kristy loved to talk to me about how God was going to use me in His work. She was such a support to me, and I miss talking to her about what the future held. I received my ordination on March 19, 2006. I remember thinking how much I wished she was there. I asked God to please let her know that I was continuing on with His work. It was so hard to move on without her.

Kristy had a sincere hunger and passion for the things of God. In other words, she walked the talk. In her own eyes, though, she always feared that she was failing God. She said to me on numerous occasions, "Dad, I just don't want to fail God." That is so opposite in much of the Christian world today. Most people think they are doing more than enough to earn heaven's reward. It really is rare to find someone whose convictions weigh so heavily upon them.

Kristy wasn't afraid to go to the altar and pour her heart out to God. She used to tell me that she just wanted to make sure things were always right between her and God. I never wanted to discourage her from doing what she felt was right in her heart. I wish more Christians would spend more time at the altar. Too many people think going to the altar is a one time journey, never to be visited again. That is just not the case, though. It is not just a place where you can receive salvation. It is a place of restitution, consecration, recognition (to say thank you), and supplication. One Sunday morning, Jonathan Blankenship, a great young preacher and man of God, made a thought-provoking statement in a message he preached at the Heritage Free Will Baptist Church, in Columbus, OH, where I attended. Brother Jonathan said, "You can tell a lot about a Christian by how often they are at the altar." That statement speaks volumes. Kristy loved going to the altar. She knew that her God would meet her there, and that was her greatest desire.

Along with working with children, Kristy's other passion was singing. She started singing in church at a very early age. To her, singing was a way to express her devotion to the One she loved so dearly. She didn't just get up on the platform and sing any song at random. She would listen to the words of a song, and when she felt that those words touched the heart of God, she would determine in her mind that was what she wanted to sing. I cannot tell you how many times I would be sitting at home and she would call me and say, "Dad, could you come down here for a minute? I have something I want you to listen to." I would walk in the house and she would be playing a particular song that spoke to her heart. She would start it over and say, "Just listen to the words, Dad. Just listen to the words." As we both listened intently, tears would come to her eyes as she thought about how that song was bringing glory to the Savior that she loved and admired so dearly. When the song ended she would say, "I'm going to learn that song and sing it in church." That is how sincere she was about her singing ministry. She prayed about every song she sang.

On April 10, 2005, Kristy sang the last song she would ever sing at the Heritage Free Will Baptist Church. Someone else was scheduled to sing that morning, but for some reason they were unable to make it. Kristy stepped in and sang, "In the Presence of Jehovah." She was sitting next to Steph and me that morning, and before she got up to sing she said, "I don't know why but I am so nervous this morning." I don't think she ever sang more beautifully than she did that morning. Four weeks later to the day she departed this life and went to be in the presence of Jehovah forevermore. It was as though God's hand was in all of the arrangements. I think it is so fitting that the words "In the Presence of Jehovah" are inscribed on Kristy's headstone. She always had a longing for the things of God. The things that she could once only imagine are now reality to her. It would be selfish of me to say that I am not happy for her.

As good as she was at everything she did, motherhood was Kristy's specialty. I would have highly recommended her as an example for any young mother who wanted to know how to raise and love a child in the proper way.

Chapter 3

A Special Mother

Her children arise up, and call her blessed
(Proverbs 31:28)

Gabe, Terryann, and Aaryn, these next few pages are especially for you. When you are old enough to understand the words that are written, here, I want you to read them carefully. They will hold great meaning to you as you one day reflect upon just how special your mom really was. Your mother loved you more than the words on these pages could ever tell, but hopefully they will give you some idea of how much you were cherished within her heart.

Her greatest desire for each one of you was that you would grow up serving God with your whole being. She wanted her life to be an example of what true Christianity really was. I hope the following words will do her memory justice for you.

Your mother was a very busy lady. That would be obvious, though, considering the fact that she was a wife and was raising four kids. It wasn't the fact that she was looking after four little ones that made her so special, though. It was the way that she did it. Even with all the constant activity in her life, she kept her priorities in order. She kept God at the center of everything she did, and she made sure that He was the center of your lives as well.

Throughout each day your mom would set aside time that was spent with each one of you individually. During that time she would read to you, color with you, play a game, or any other number of things. Her point was to make sure that each of you knew that you could count on her. It was her special time alone with you. Gabe and Terryann, I don't know if you can remember any of those times or not, but I do remember how you looked so forward to it. I would walk into your house and one of you would say, "It's my turn to spend special time with mommy."

The remarkable thing about this was the fact that your mother always took time for her own daily devotions and prayer time as well. Even though she came to realize that her greatest ministry was caring for her own family, she never failed to see the importance of spending quality time alone with God herself. She knew that was where her strength lied. It would have been so easy to steal a nap when the opportunity presented itself but she told me that was the perfect time to read and pray. She took advantage of her quiet moments when they presented themselves.

Gabe, Terryann, and Aaryn, right now I want to share some personal thoughts which prove the undying love and devotion your mother had for each one of you.

Gabe:

You have your mom's wit and sense of humor. She liked to laugh, joke, and have a good time, and she loved being around people. You have all of those same qualities. Your mom would get so tickled at the funny things you would do, and the more she would laugh, the more you would keep it up.

She used to sit and read to you all the time. When you were small you enjoyed that more than anything. She especially liked reading to you from your Bible Stories For Children book. She was always amazed at the way you would remember in detail the stories she read to you. When Mam Maw and I would come to your house she always wanted you to tell us what you had learned out of the Bible. She would say, "Isn't that something? Gabe probably knows more about the Bible than most adults." Your mother always told me that she thought God had His hand on your life in a special way.

As you were getting older she knew that she was at a disadvantage because you were already starting to get interested in sports. It was easy to keep the girls happy by playing dolls with them, but you wanted to pass ball, shoot baskets, or play kick ball. Your mom was the first one to admit that athletics was never her field of expertise. That never stopped her from trying though.

It wasn't uncommon for me to look out my back door and see her trying to pass ball or attempting to play basketball with you to the best of her ability. She may have not been into sports but she sure loved watching you play. I remember how she looked so forward to watching you play baseball. Your first year of playing was 2005. The accident that took her and Dani's lives happened before your season actually began. She was at your practices that you had before the accident. One thing is for sure. She would have been to every game that you played. There was nothing you, Terryann, or Dani ever did that she wasn't right there with you.

Your mother was so proud of you, and she always said, "Gabe is so smart. He can do anything that he puts his mind to." If it was only coloring a picture, telling a Bible story, or making a basket, she was just proud of the fact that you were her son.

She said to me one time, "Gabe is too smart. He can't be easily fooled." You proved just how right she was one particular Christmas. You were three at the time. She had ordered you two books with pictures of cars in them. You always loved looking at old cars. It was getting close to Christmas and she was worried that the books wouldn't get there in time. One day when she and I were talking she said to me, "The C-A-R B-O-O-K-S haven't got here yet. I sure hope they get here in time." She spelled out the words "car books" to make sure that you weren't aware of this special present she wanted to surprise you with.

As fate would have it, the books did arrive a few days before Christmas. Mam Maw and I were there that Christmas morning as all of you were opening your presents. Your mom loved watching all of you at Christmas. She just loved seeing that you were happy. We were watching as you opened the car books. When you saw what they were you jumped up excitedly and said, "My car books, I knew they would get here in time!" She laughed so hard about that. I am so glad that I have that special moment on video. She thought there was no way that you knew anything about those books. Not only did you know about them, but you also kept it a secret that you knew. To her, you keeping the secret was the amazing thing. Again, she said, "Gabe is just too smart."

Gabe, I know that you were only six when your mother died, and over the years memories may fade. Hold onto and cherish those memories that you do have. You cannot possibly know how much your mom loved you. I hope this book will in some way allow you to always keep her in your heart until you see her again. She is in heaven waiting for you, Terryann, and Aaryn. The next time you see your mom you will be with her forever.

Terryann:

You have your mom's gift to sing. Even before you could talk you would move your body to the beat of music when you heard it. It may have only been a commercial on television, but you always moved with the music. Your mom would get so tickled at watching you. She always said that you would one day sing in church, and she looked so forward to that day.

She loved taking you for walks. Until you were able to ride your bike she would push you around the block in your stroller. To you, it didn't matter what she did, as long as she was spending time with you. I can remember how she would get down on the floor and play Barbie dolls with you. She even did that when she was pregnant with Aaryn.

One Christmas your mommy and Mam Maw built you a huge doll house. When you stood up it was taller than you. They spent hours and hours working on that doll house, making all the curtains and decorations for it. She was so excited about giving it to you. She could hardly wait. Believe me, she got more joy out of giving you that doll house than you did in receiving it. She loved seeing you smile. When you were happy, your mom was happy. When you were sad, she was sad.

One of her favorite things she liked to do with all of you was take you to the library. She patiently let you pick out the books you wanted. Then she would take you home and read them to you. One time when you were in pre-school your teacher taught the class a few sign language gestures. You became real interested in that. Your mom found a book on sign language and started learning it herself. Then she started teaching you. We would all be sitting at the dinner table, and both of you would sign words to one another. It was something special that only you and her shared.

You were never a selfish child. Whatever you did, you were always patient to wait your turn. You were always willing to even give some of your toys to other kids who had less than you. Your mom always said that if God ever called any of her kids into the mission field it would be you. She always prayed that your unselfish spirit would remain with you as you got older.

Mommy enrolled you in pre-school during the 2004-2005 school year. Around February 2005 she decided to remove you and keep you at home with her. She said she wanted to be able to spend more alone time with you. Gabe was in school all day, so when Dani and Aaryn went down for a nap she took advantage of that time for just you and her. Looking back on that we have been able to see God's hand in that whole situation. You see, it was only about three month's later that the accident happened and your mom went to be with Jesus. During those three month's I believe the two of you made a special bond that will last forever. You may not even realize it, yet, but in time you will.

Terryann, I will tell you what I told Gabe. You were both very young when you lost your mom. You were only five years old at the time. I know that memories will become harder and harder to hold on to, but hold tightly to those that you do have. For the longest time, you didn't want to talk about Mommy or Dani. You said that it made you sad. I know that it was the saddest thing that ever happened to you honey. You just keep believing what Mam Maw and I tell you all the time: your mother loved you so much more than words could ever say, and she is now in heaven waiting for you. You will see her and Dani again.

Until that day, never forget how much she loved you. You were so special to her. I know that if she could say anything to you it would be, "I am waiting for you Terryann. I wish you could see how beautiful heaven is. One day, we will sit down together again, just you and I, and it will be as though we were never apart."

Mam Maw and I will always be here for you Terryann. We love you and we are so proud of you, just like your mother was. One day we will all be together again.

Aaryn:

You were only eight months old when your mother died, so you undoubtedly have no recollection of her at all or of how much she loved you. I will say the same thing to you that I said to Gabe and Terryann: it would be impossible to put into words how much she loved and cared for you. By the time a fourth child is born the newness has already worn off in most instances, but that certainly wasn't true where your mommy was concerned. She was just as excited about giving birth to you as she was Gabe, Terryann, or Dani. Each one of you were special to her in your own way.

I remember how your mom would hold you close to her and sing to you. It was never a chore or a burden for her to get up in the middle of the night to feed you or look after you. To her it was just another opportunity to bond with you.

She used to say that she was so blessed because God gave her the most beautiful children in the world. She had a family portrait taken at Christmas of 2004. In one of the pictures it shows your mom holding you in her arms and gazing into your eyes. You can just look at that picture and she how much she loved and cared for you.

Even though you were only eight months old, Mommy spent so much quality time with you as well. At some time throughout the day she would just hold you and sing to you or talk to you like you could understand everything she was saying. Whenever you would give even the smallest hint of a smile she would just glow with pride. While fixing dinner or watching after your brother or sisters she would set you in the baby swing. Mommy always bragged about how you were such a good baby to just sit there and swing as you watched all the happenings around you.

One day your mom brought you down to our house and said she wanted to show us something. "I have the smartest baby in the world, and I can prove it to you," she said. She had these little socks on your feet that had the day of the week written on them. She said, "Ask Aaryn what day it is." So, we humored her and asked you what day it was. Then Mommy, holding you in her lap took your little feet and lifted them up toward us and joyfully exclaimed, "It's Thursday," showing us that you had the answer written on the bottoms of your socks. "See, didn't I tell you that my baby was the smartest baby in the world." Then she would give you a big hug. We have your mother on video doing this with you and I'm so glad that we captured that special moment.

Aaryn, though you may have no memories of your own, there are lots of things left behind to let you know what kind of person your mother was and just how much she loved you. The CD of her singing, the videos, the pictures, and the articles written about her are priceless. We even have letters written specifically to you from many of the young mothers in our church who were touched by your mom's life. They too wanted you to know how much your mom meant to them and the love she had for you. I hope that each of those things will in some small way be a reflection to you of the love and special qualities she possessed.

I believe there is an endless bond that exists between a mother and her child that is formed as the mother is carrying that little one. Though they may be separated by circum-stances in life, I don't believe even death itself can break that eternal bond. There is something down deep within each one of their beings which allows them to know there was something special that they once had. It is a void that is only temporal for those who know God and His eternal plan of salvation. That bond will one day be complete again.

Aaryn, I hope these few words have touched your heart in some way. Since you were so young when your mom died you never had to experience the life changes that Gabe and Terryann did. I suppose everything that happened after that must have just seemed natural to you, whereas they both had to adjust to life without their mom. I know your mom would want you to be happy, and your happiness is what Mam Maw and I pray for. One day you will be reunited with your mother again. Then all of us will live together forever in the joys of the Lord. Until that day please know that Mam Maw and I will always be here for you. Mam Maw and I loved your mom and your sister Dani so much, and we miss them greatly. We love you, Gabe, and Terryann just as we did them.

****

Kristy had four children, and she loved each one of them equally. She once said to me that she didn't know how any parent ever dealt with the loss of a child. She had a miscarriage between having Dani and Aaryn. She had a hard time dealing with that, and I'm not really sure that she ever got over it. When Dani died that Sunday afternoon, May 1, 2005, we worried about how we would tell Kristy when she got better. God chose to take care of it another way. Seven days later, on Mothers' Day, He also brought Kristy home, and mother and daughter were together again. I'd be lying if I said that I hadn't questioned God numerous times, but I know that He has good reasons for all that He does and allows to happen. I kept remembering all those times when Kristy said she didn't know if she would ever be able to bear the burden of losing a child. Maybe she wouldn't have been able to bear it, and God was just keeping His promise that He made in 1 Corinthians 10:13: *"God is faithful; he will not let you be tempted (tried) beyond what you can bear."* That is the kind of heavenly Father we serve. He always keeps His promises.

****

Final thoughts:

Simply put, Kristy was the best person I ever knew. She wanted to make a difference in the lives of everyone she came in contact with. Her actions and motives for everything she did were pure and honest. Her relationship with God can best be described as sincere and genuine. Kristy was a devoted wife to her husband Matthew. She loved him with all of her heart. As you have already read, her children meant everything to her. Her mother and I could not be prouder than to have known her as our daughter. We thank God for the twenty-seven years He allowed us to have her in our lives.

I miss Kristy more than words could ever tell. I miss her laughter and her smile. I miss her wit and humor. I miss the way she would call me at work and say, "I just wanted to say hi." I miss hearing her say "I love you". I miss watching her play with her kids. I miss hearing her sing. I miss talking about the Bible with her. I miss going out to lunch with her. You see, Kristy was more than a daughter to me. She was also a friend. As much as I miss her, though, I wouldn't bring her back even if I could. I love her too much to do that to her, because she is now at peace in the presence of Jehovah. One day I will see her and Dani again. What a glorious day that will be!

I hope what you have read in this chapter will help you to better understand just how special Kristy was. Every time I listen to her CD I am reminded of what she always said to

me, "Just listen to the words Dad. Just listen to the words."
Kristy loved to sing, but even more importantly, she loved
the One about whom she was singing. Those things that she
could once only imagine are now reality to her.

Chapter 4

"Dani"

But Jesus said, Suffer little children, and forbid
them not, to come unto me; for of such is the
kingdom of heaven.
(Matthew 19:14)

There is a very popular cartoon strip called Garfield. I'm sure that you've seen it before. If so, you know there are three main characters to the cartoon. First of course, there is Garfield. He is a lazy, selfish, overweight, orange tabby cat whose only ambition in life is to eat and sleep. Next, there is Jon, who is Garfield's owner, although it is actually Jon who answers to the whims of his arrogant little feline. Then there is Odie. Odie is a little floppy eared dog who has more energy than a lightning storm. His rambunctious and constant jumping and hopping around makes Garfield tired just watching him. Odie loves everyone and only wants to run and play. If I were going to compare our little Dani to a cartoon character it would be Odie, hands down. She was a power-packed bundle of energy who never seemed to tire. She would run and play until she just fizzled out on her own with exhaustion. Dani would be playing with everything that was in her little body one moment, and then you would walk in her room and see her laying in her bed, or even on the floor with her blanket fast asleep. As soon as she woke up the whole procedure started all over again.

It's a well known fact that most children are blessed with more than enough energy. How many times have we said, "I wish I just had a portion of what they have," or "if you could bottle up their energy and sell it you would be a millionaire." Thank God for children. They do one of two things to us: They help keep us young, or they help us age quicker.

I kid you not, though, when I say that Dani seemed to have energy extraordinaire. That child never stopped. As great as heaven has to be, I believe it to be an even livelier place now with Dani there.

Her non-stop action often got her into trouble as she would eventually cross the proverbial line that all parents draw in order to maintain some kind of sanity in the home. I can't tell you how many times I would walk into Matt and Kristy's house and see Dani standing in the corner facing the wall with arms extended toward heaven She would turn around long enough to smile at Mam Maw or me, tell us hi, and gesture as if to say, "I'll be out of here in no time. Just wait a minute and I'll come over there and give you a big hug." I have often kidded in saying that when Dani entered heaven it was the first day that she did not have to spend some portion of that day standing in a corner!

Wherever she was, Dani was the center of attention. She didn't try to be. That was just her personality. I remember one Sunday morning after church we were standing in the foyer talking. All of a sudden here comes Dani running out of junior church. I'm not sure what she learned that morning but she began running in huge circles around the foyer screaming out all the while, "I'm the devil, I'm the devil." Between the startled looks and chuckles from those now looking on I'm trying to stop her before her mom and dad see her, because I just know that somehow I am going to get blamed for this. That was just Dani. You never knew what to expect out of her. She got a notion, and she just did it.

Though she was three years younger than Gabe, and nineteen months younger than Terryann, Dani had no problem holding her own with her older siblings. There were times when they would all be wrestling on the floor together and Dani never gave an inch. I have videos of them playing like that together, and I wouldn't take a million dollars for those precious memories.

She loved Gabe and Terryann immensely. Though she enjoyed playing Barbie dolls with her big sister, it wasn't uncommon to see her playing cars with Gabe. Dani was easily amused, and though she liked being with her brother and sister, and other kids as well, she was also content to play alone. Steph and I fixed up our basement living room into a huge playroom for the kids. When they were smaller Gabe and Terryann never liked being down there alone, but Dani would be content to stay there for long periods of time by herself while playing and singing. She just loved life to its fullest.

She never feared anything. It was wonderful living just two doors down from my grandkids, but it was also cause for worry. Kristy always used to tell me that I worried too much. I would look out my back door and see Dani hanging upside down from their playhouse. In desperation, I would run out into the yard and tell her to get down from there before she fell. She would just laugh and do it all the more.

Whenever the kids were out in the backyard playing and they would see me or Steph outside, they would yell for us to come over and see them. I would always go over to the fence, lift them up and give them a hug. It got to where Gabe and Terryann were getting too big to lift but Dani was still small enough. If I would lift her up and set her down on our side of the fence she would take off for the house to see Mam Maw.

Dani was constantly changing her clothes. She would often change five or six times a day. Some of the outfits she put on were hilarious. Kristy used to just take it all in stride. She would say to me, "Dad, you have to pick your battles. As long as she is having a good time that's all that matters."

I remember one time when I walked into their house Dani was wearing the most bizarre outfit that you could ever imagine. Get this now: she had on a little pair of sweat pants, a shirt that didn't match, and a swim suit over top of it. She topped off her fashion statement in a pair of snow boots. I looked at Kristy and said, "Do you see her?" She said, "What?" "Look at what she has on!" I said in disbelief. As nonchalantly as she could, Kristy said, "She does that all the time. You have to pick your battles, Dad." Eventually we all learned to expect anything out of her. She was full of surprises.

Dani was definitely mommy's girl, so everyone worried about how she would handle it when Aaryn was born. That question was soon answered after mommy and new baby arrived home from the hospital. Dani made over Aaryn even more than Gabe and Terryann did. In fact, you had to make sure that Aaryn wasn't left in the room alone with her. I remember one time when we walked into the living room and there was Dani trying to lift Aaryn out of the baby swing. She wanted to help feed her, change her, and she even wanted to help Kristy bathe her. She would jump up beside of Kristy onto the couch and say, "Can I hold Aaryn, now?" She was so proud of her little sister.

Still though, when she wasn't feeling well Dani wanted her mommy. She was still mommy's girl, and in her way she let everyone know that. As much as I miss them both I am so happy for them. Dani preceded her mommy in heaven by seven days and I'm sure that when Kristy walked into her new home Dani was there to meet her. I often picture the two of them walking side by side, hand in hand, down a path surrounded by beautiful trees and flowers. I can see Dani running and playing while Kristy looks upon her with a peace, joy, and contentment that can only be experienced in heaven. Truly, we have so much to look forward to experiencing.

Dani loved everything about church, but I believe her favorite part of it was Pioneer Club. Pioneer Club is the Wednesday night program for the kids. Even at just three years old she enjoyed learning the Scripture verses and singing new songs. Her favorite song was "Thy Word is a Lamp Unto My Feet." She used to sing it all the time. As a matter of fact, Matt had that verse put on her headstone. I can just imagine her playing in heaven while singing that little chorus.

Final Thoughts:

I often wonder what Dani will look like the next time I see her. Will I see her as I remembered her while on Earth, or will she be an adult? I'm not sure that anyone has the answer to that question. Those are things we don't have to worry about, though, because our God knows how to make everything its absolute best.

I miss that little girl more than I can put into words. I miss watching her play in the back yard. I miss her climbing the fence and running into my arms. I miss the way she got so excited at opening presents on Christmas day. I miss hearing her sing. I miss the smell of her hair, her little cheek against mine, and hearing her say, "I love you, Pap Paw." Though

God took Dani at just the tender age of three, she left behind a multitude of memories. She will never be forgotten.

I thank God for the three years that He let us have her. As much as it hurts to think about how she departed this life so tragically, I would have rather had those three short years than to have not known her at all. It just makes the thought of heaven that much sweeter.

Chapter 5

A Tragic Day

*For my thoughts are not your thoughts, neither are
your ways my ways, saith the Lord.*
(Isaiah 55:8)

May 1, 2005, started out like every other Sunday morning in our household. Steph and I got to church early and waited out in the foyer to meet the grandkids before they scurried off to their respective Sunday School classes. That was pretty much our normal routine. We would give them a hug and then head off to our own class. I felt blessed to have my wife, daughter, and son-in-law in the Sunday School class that I taught. I had no idea that particular morning would be the last time my daughter would ever hear me teach.

That morning I taught from Jeremiah 1:5. I ask you to intently read that verse of Scripture right now. *"Before I formed thee in the belly, I knew thee; and before thou camest forth out of the womb I sanctified thee, and I ordained thee a prophet unto the nations."* Of course, the Lord was talking to Jeremiah, but the implication from this verse applies to all of God's children. What is that implication I'm talking about? Our God knows everything about us. He knows our past, He knows our present circumstances, and He knows what lies ahead. He is the One who formed and laid out the plans for our individual lives. Nothing takes our Heavenly Father by surprise. There has never been one event that has ever transpired in your or my life when God had to step back and say, "Wow, I never saw that coming!" The divine potter is continually and skillfully at work preparing us for the unforeseen things which lie before us. In His plan, God ordained you and me to do a particular work for Him, just as much as He ordained Jeremiah. Jeremiah felt inadequate to perform the task God was asking him to do. Just as God had to deal with Jeremiah's feelings of inadequacy, so does He also deal with ours. Our God knows just what we need, and His timing is never wrong.

That was the crux of my lesson that morning. I have often looked back and marveled at some of the things that I said and taught that morning. I can see how my study and preparation for that week's lesson would be essential for the coming days that I would be facing. God had spoken to my heart all week about how He was the One in total control of my life. That was the message I tried to convey to my class that morning. God taught me that week what I was going to need for what was about to transpire in my life.

On Tuesday, July 27, 2004, at 2:30 am, I accepted God's call upon my life to go into the ministry. This was after many weeks of running, praying, and toiling in the Spirit. When at last I told the Lord that I accepted His call upon my life, it was like a great weight fell from my shoulders. I often likened it to the same feeling I experienced at the time of my conversion. There is no greater feeling than to know you are in God's perfect will. Kristy was so excited for me. She was such an encouragement and was always wanting to talk with me about how the Lord might possibly want to use me in His service. I miss the way she would just want to sit and talk about God and the Scriptures. I've often wondered if she knew just how much I valued and trusted her opinion on spiritual issues. Though she was young in years she had a knowledge and wisdom for the things of God that was only superseded by her love for Him.

I ended that morning's Sunday School lesson by talking about the beginning of Christ's ministry in the Gospel of Matthew. I made the statement that at that point man was about to enter the age of grace. What I would later come to understand was that God's grace is far greater and reaches much farther than we as humans can even begin to realize. There really is an irony to God's grace. It is so simple, yet complex at the same time. The simplicity of God's saving grace reaches out to every person born into this world. This remarkable grace makes itself known in an undeniable way to the receptive and seeking heart, yet at the same time this same grace escapes the knowledge of the greatest of human minds. As simple as God's saving grace is to accept and understand, the complexity of His grace which carries us through every trial or problem that we encounter in this life is unexplainable, yet so very real to the life and spirit of the one walking in it. I can truly testify to the simplicity and complexity of such grace, as He has carried me when I could just go no farther on my own. John Newton certainly knew what He was writing about when he penned "Amazing Grace."

After that morning's church service, we all went to lunch together. I am so thankful for that last hour we spent together as a complete family. I sat across from Dani, and as usual I spent a great deal of my time trying to keep her in her seat. If I would have allowed her she would have just wandered throughout the restaurant seeing what she could get into. She has now been with the Lord for over two years and I wouldn't be surprised to learn that she hasn't sat down yet! I have often thought that once her little feet touched her new home she probably took off running.

As we got up to leave the restaurant we gave our customary good-bye hugs and said, "We'll see you at the evening service in a few hours." We just had such a good time that afternoon, and the thought of that being the last time we would enjoy each others' company as a whole family was the farthest thing from my mind. I have often thought since then how we really do tend to take so much for granted.

Matt, Kristy, and the kids were going to her Grandma's house and would later go over to her Aunt Karin's to see her aunt's nursery. Though Karin was Kristy's aunt they were only five months apart in age. They grew up together and were more like sisters. Karin was expecting her first child and was so excited to show her new nursery to Kristy.

Steph and I went to church that evening and as usual, we waited to greet the kids before going into the service. When it came time for the service to start and they still hadn't shown up we began to get worried. In fact, there was a gnawing, almost sickening feeling inside both Steph and myself that something was wrong. It may have been pure parental instinct, but we also knew our daughter. Even though Kristy was a twenty-seven year old married woman with four kids, she still always respected us enough to call if she wasn't going to be somewhere where we expected her to be. We knew that if for some reason she wouldn't be at church that evening she would call. We just knew something wasn't right. I certainly didn't want to panic, but I can still remember that awful feeling that let me know something terrible was wrong.

We went to the church office and began trying to track them down. Steph called her mom and sister to see if they knew anything. Her mom confirmed that they had been there and left for Karin's, but Karin said they never showed up. By now Steph and I both were starting to panic. Steph tried calling Kristy's cell phone but there was no answer.

We called our voice mail at home and our suspicions became reality. The Highway Patrol had left a message that told us our family had been in an automobile accident. They were very vague with the details saying only that there was a wreck. I called the Highway Patrol. I told the lady there who I was and that there was a message left on my voice mail about the accident. With a knot in my stomach and afraid of what I was going to hear, I asked her, "Ma'am, were there any fatalities?" The hesitation in her voice answered my worst suspicions. She asked me how I was related to them. I told her the family in the van was my daughter, son-in-law, and grandkids. I begged her again to please tell me what she knew. She said, "Sir, you need to call Berger Hospital. That is all I can tell you." As I hung up the phone my mind was absolutely numb. The thought of what I knew to be true was more than I could seem to handle at that moment. I knew that at least one, if not more, in my family was dead. One by one each of them passed through my mind; I wondered if it was Gabe, Terryann, Dani, or Aaryn. Was it Kristy or Matt? By this time my thought process was out of control and I hardly knew what was even going on around me.

During those moments the church service, which had already started, was interrupted to let the congregation know what had just happened. Someone had called the necessary sources and found out the details. The irony of every event which transpired during that time and the following week is that, as confused as my mind was, they are still as fresh as though they happened yesterday. Steph and I experienced things over those next few days that will never leave us.

Our youth pastor, Chris Mitchell, called Steph and I, along with Matt's parents, into the pastor's office and told us to sit down. I remember thinking how I had to know what had happened but I didn't think I was ready to hear it. Pastor Chris started out by saying that Dani had died at the scene of the accident and Kristy had been life-flighted to Grant

Hospital in Columbus. I honestly don't know what else was said after that. I completely lost it. I should have been there holding my wife and supporting her through the greatest ordeal of her life but I just absolutely broke down in my own grief. I stood up, took a few steps, and then fell to the floor. I felt as if my whole world had just fallen apart.

As I lay there sobbing, I cried out to God in desperation wondering how I would ever survive this terrible tragedy. I recalled His promise that He would not allow us to go through anything that we were not able to bear. At that moment I honestly thought I had gone beyond that point.

There is an irony in the things of God which cannot be explained or understood by human reasoning. One has to experience the greatest of pain before they can experience the greatest of grace. When we were told that Dani had died, I totally fell apart. Even at that moment though, I felt God's touch. I cried out to God, "I can't take this," He said to me, "I know you can't, but I can."

I can't explain it. It can only be understood through the work of the Holy Spirit. Philippians 4:7 talks about *"the peace of God, which passes all understanding."* I had just received the worst news that I thought I could ever hear. As I lay there in confusion and apparent hopelessness, suddenly the peace of God passed through me like a gentle breeze on a warm, sunny day. There are no words to describe the pain that I felt. I knew this was something that I wouldn't get over in just a few days; yet, I felt the peace of God that assured me He was there. I knew at that moment He was carrying me. I found His Word to be true, that He would never leave me nor forsake me. Since the accident I have come to learn a lot about God's grace, and it all started that moment, as I lay there crying on my pastor's office floor.

My pastor, Tim Stout, and his wife, Tobianne, drove Steph and me to the hospital. I was in no condition to drive.

Honestly, at that time I'm not sure I could have found my own way home. I wasn't in shock but I was certainly in a state of numbness. My head was spinning while grieving for Dani, wondering if Kristy was going to make it, and how Matt and the others kids were. There was so much to think about and I just couldn't grasp all of it.

When we got to the hospital they told us Kristy was in surgery. About two hours later the doctor came out and told us that she was in very bad condition. They said the next twenty-four hours were critical. She had lost an enormous amount of blood and had received serious wounds to her liver, lungs, and kidneys. She had so much going against her. Her liver was cut so badly that they couldn't stop the bleeding. The doctors were openly honest with us and said Kristy's chances for survival weren't very good. We knew that we needed to pray for a miracle. We later learned that Christians nationwide were praying with us. Our church was unbelievably supportive toward us during this crisis in our lives.

The next seven days proved to be the most mentally draining time of our lives. It was an emotional roller coaster ride. Though the situation was bleak, to say the least, we were hanging onto anything positive the doctors would tell us. Every time one thing would improve, something else would get worse. It was so mentally exhausting and I felt so helpless. Again, though, I want to testify to the indescribable grace of God. As tired, confused, and scared as I was, I could feel His ever-abiding presence.

While trying to remain at Kristy's bedside as much as possible, we still had Matt and the other three kids to think about as well. Matt's injuries were the worst among the rest of them. He had a broken left arm, fractured left hip, and several cuts to his face, arms, and legs. He was at Grant Hospital along with Kristy, so that made communication with him much easier. The next day Matt had surgery to have a plate, pins, and screws inserted to repair his badly broken left arm. He was admitted on the sixth floor. Kristy was in the third floor trauma unit. Matt wasn't released until Thursday, so in the meantime we would go back and forth between floors letting him know what was going on with Kristy. It wasn't actually until Wednesday of that week that he even got to visit her.

I talked extensively with Matt about the accident. He said that it happened so quickly that they hardly even had time to react. Kristy was driving, and they had to take a detour on their way to her Aunt Karin's house. They were on an unfamiliar back road. She pulled out in front of another vehicle and was broadsided. They were only a little more than a mile from Karin's house. Karin later told us that she heard all the sirens and the helicopter but had no idea it was Kristy. The van they drove was turned over on its side. After I saw pictures of the accident I was surprised that any of them survived. The driver and two children in the other car were all right, so we were very thankful for that as well.

Dani's little neck was broken on impact. They transported her, Matt, and Gabe to Berger Hospital, which was about 30 minutes south of downtown Columbus. Terryann and Aaryn were taken to Children's Hospital in Columbus. Before Matt was transferred to Grant Hospital they brought Dani to him and let him hold her. They cut off a little lock of her hair and gave it to him. I am so thankful that the Lord chose to take her instantly rather than allow her to lay and suffer. She could not have known what even hit her.

Of the three other children, Aaryn had the most severe injuries. Her liver had a small laceration, and the doctors had some problems controlling the bleeding. She was able to be released from Children's Hospital by Tuesday afternoon, though. She had a lot of internal bruising. It was so pitiful to watch her as she would just lay there and whimper. She was so bruised that it hurt her just to be picked up.

Terryann was treated and released with a severe stressed neck and back. She had to be in a neck brace for about four weeks. Gabe was treated and released with a broken left leg.

It was a very trying and exhausting week to say the least. Steph and I spent the first few days running from the third floor to the sixth floor at Grant Hospital. We would then go over to Children's Hospital to visit Aaryn. Then we tried to make ample time to spend with Gabe and Terryann, who were staying with Matt's uncle and aunt. We were trying to hide from Gabe and Terryann that their little sister had died and how badly injured their mommy was. Hiding these facts from them was ripping me apart inside. How would we tell them? I dreaded the thought of them experiencing the same pain that I was feeling inside. To be quite honest, I guess I underestimated the ability of God's grace to reach out to His little ones as well as us adults.

Later in the week I made the comment that we were so busy running to and fro that I felt like I didn't have the proper time I needed to sufficiently grieve for Dani. One evening Steph and I went home to shower and grab a couple of hours sleep. As we sat in our living room, we held pictures of our little granddaughter in our laps and just cried with one another. How would we ever get over this tragic loss of our little Dani? Words cannot describe the pain that comes with the death of a loved one who was so much a vital part of your life. Whenever I hear of a parent or grandparent losing a child my heart just aches for them.

My church was so supportive during this time. Steph and I practically lived at the hospital that last week of Kristy's life. There were very few moments that we were ever there alone. Someone was always there with us, and many times there were several of our brothers and sisters in Christ there supporting us and praying for us. As we waited for what seemed like countless hours, the waiting room was often taken over by our family and members of the Heritage Free Will Baptist Church. We later learned that the huge outpouring of support from our church was the talk of the hospital. As much as I tried to express my gratitude to those precious people I don't believe they will ever begin to realize how much that meant to Steph and me.

Even before Kristy was out of surgery that Sunday evening, the waiting room was filled with people not only from our church but also other churches. One by one, they hugged us, prayed with us, and comforted us as best they could. Honestly, there are no words that can be spoken which can even begin to remotely make any sense during a time like that. No one there tried to make any sense out of it with some meaningless theological answer. If someone would have tried to give an answer as to why our little Dani had to die and why Kristy was now fighting for her life, it simply wouldn't have mattered at that moment. I often stated that the only two comments which registered with me at all that week were, "I'm praying for you," or "I just don't know what to say." It was nothing spiritual or profound, yet those simple words spoke volumes to our grieving hearts. They were words filled with concern, care, and compassion, coming from people who loved us so much that they were sharing our pain and burden with us. Nothing is more precious to a grieving heart than to know someone cares.

There were so many people there that Sunday night that I couldn't even begin to name all of them. I certainly don't want to recognize one individual any more than another for what that meant to us, but I do have to tell of one particular moment that deeply touched me. I was sitting down, my eyes filled with tears, just trying to collect my thoughts and make some sense of all that was happening. I felt a hand reach out and touch me just as had happened so many previous times that evening. I looked up and saw two people that touched my heart as no one else could have that night. It was Bill and Angie Fitzpatrick.

In August 1995, Bill and Angie's three year old daughter, Jamie was also killed in an automobile accident. When I looked up and saw Bill and Angie I can't put into words what that did for my broken heart. They didn't have to say anything. Just knowing that they understood the pain Steph and I were now going through somehow made it more bearable. I know that God sent them there to us that evening. At moments such as these you find yourself searching for anything that can even remotely bring some inner peace. Being with someone else that you know has also experienced the same pain really does bring a sense of comfort that cannot be explained. I think it greatly hinges on the fact that having seen how they have survived such an ordeal gives you hope that somehow, someway, you will get through it as well. There is a definite bond between people that have been through the same kind of tragedies. It is a bond that brings unity between individuals. Their unity is not founded in spoken words, but rather in the pain that embraces them. It really is a fraternity that I wish no one else would ever have to join.

For all of my brothers and sisters in Christ who were there that night, I hope you understand the things I just wrote about Bill and Angie. This is not to say that their presence meant more to me than anyone else's. Steph and I so much appreciate each and every person who sacrificed many hours, not only that Sunday evening but also every day and night that following week to sit and be with us.

Chapter 6

A Week of Darkness

For thou art my lamp, O Lord: and the Lord will
lighten my darkness.
(2 Samuel 22:29)

God used the following week to prepare our hearts to let go of Kristy. He knows what is best. Some may wonder why He didn't just take her with Dani if His intentions were to bring her home anyway. Those are questions to which only He has the answers. I do believe this, though: when God chooses to bring one of His children home, His focus then turns to those who are left behind. It may have been that to lose Kristy and Dani both on that same day would have been too much for us to bear. Or, He may have had to take Dani in order for us to have the peace we needed to let go of Kristy. As hard as it was, there was a comfort in knowing that, a week later, mommy and daughter were reunited together again. One comes to the realization that all you have to stand on is your faith, regardless of how much it may dwindle during these kinds of trying times. God does know what is best for each and every one of us. His plans which are for our good go so far beyond our logic, reasoning, and understanding. Isaiah 55:8 says, *"For my thoughts are*

*not your thoughts, neither are your ways my ways, saith the
Lord.*" That pretty much says it all, don't you think?

Monday, May 2

The doctors had told us that the first twenty-four hours
were critical, so Steph and I stayed all night at the hospital.
Kristy lost an extreme amount of blood, and they were
concerned about her blood platelet level. They explained to
us that platelets help the blood to clot and stop the bleeding.
The enormous amount of blood loss affected Kristy's platelet
level significantly. The doctors were very honest with us
from the start. They told us that, when a person's platelet
level drops as low as Kristy's, it is rare that they would
survive. We knew that we needed a miracle. Within just a
few hours, churches and other Christians from all over the
country were being notified about Kristy, and people started
praying. Anyone who had family members from other states
called and had their congregations praying. We even received
word that Christians from other countries were praying with
us. If you have never been there, I have to tell you that it is
an unexplainable feeling to know that brothers and sisters
in Christ that you don't even personally know are binding
together with you in prayer in your most desperate hour of
need.

Kristy was conscious that afternoon. She wasn't able
to talk because of the tube in her throat but she did write
messages in my hand. I would ask her a question and she
would write out the answer with her finger. We were careful
about what we told her. She knew that she had been in an
automobile accident and that she was in the hospital. Of
course, we didn't tell her anything about Dani. We told her
that Matt was in a room upstairs and that Uncle Jimmy and
Aunt Jean were watching the kids. I'm not sure if she really
believed us or not. I've often wondered if she thought some
of them died from the crash and we just weren't telling her.

I'm so glad that she was conscious that afternoon. That would be the last time that we would communicate with Kristy where we knew for sure she understood us. We told her that we loved her and to please keep fighting for Matt and the kids. I asked her if she knew how much her mom and dad loved her. She squeezed my hand ever so gently as her strength would allow as if to say, "I know you do, and I love you too." I will always cherish that moment. Shortly afterwards Kristy became very restless and they put her in an induced coma. She never did regain consciousness again.

Kristy was only breathing about fifty percent on her own. They still couldn't get her liver to stop bleeding and they had to raise her heart rate in hopes of keeping all of her other organs working properly.

We didn't want to leave but we knew we had Matt and the kids to think about as well. We went up to the sixth floor to see how Matt was doing. We continually kept him informed of what was happening with Kristy. We then slipped over to Children's Hospital to see Aaryn. She was going to be all right, but the small laceration on her little liver made her very sore, as well as all of the internal bruising. It was so sad as she would quietly whimper at even the most gentle touch from anyone. Even though she was only eight months old I'm sure she must have wondered where her mommy was, who cradled her so close to her body as no one else possibly could have.

After leaving Children's Hospital we went over to Uncle Jimmy and Aunt Jean's to see Gabe and Terryann. Gabe had his leg in a cast, and Terryann had to wear a neck brace but they were both fine. Naturally, they had many questions, and I'm sure they were a bit scared, but I sometimes think kids are tougher than we think. Still though, I wondered how we would ever tell them about their little sister. How would we explain to them that their mommy wasn't going to come home if Kristy did die? It was almost too much to think about at that moment. Our whole world had been turned upside down in just a matter of twenty-four hours, and I was having trouble just collecting my thoughts.

That night as we lay in bed trying to get a few hours sleep Steph asked me how we would be able to continue on if Kristy died. I took her in my arms and said that I didn't think there was any way God would take her. We had already lost Dani. I really expected a miracle because I honestly didn't believe that God would take Kristy, too. He said that He would put no more on us than we could bear, and I truly didn't think we could bear the loss of our daughter, as well as our granddaughter. We finally fell asleep from exhaustion but were awake once again in just a few hours.

Tuesday, May 3

We got up early Tuesday morning and went straight to the hospital. The doctors made their rounds early and we always made sure we were there to talk with them to see if there were any changes in Kristy's condition.

Kristy actually had a bit of a setback during the night. We got used to hearing that throughout the next few days. We were hanging on to every bit of hope that we could find. We weren't looking day-to-day, but rather hour-to-hour. One hour something would change that made us think things were improving. Then the next hour it seemed that she would have another setback. It really did become an emotional roller coaster ride.

The doctors kept Kristy's heart rate increased to about 140-150. That is very high when you consider the average human heart rate is 70-80. They actually kept it that high for that whole week. One of the doctors told us that had she been a smoker or much older her heart would have never lasted that long at that rate. Because she was so young and in good health, though, they were able to maintain the increased heart rate.

She was still only breathing about fifty percent on her own. They still couldn't get her liver to stop bleeding and they had to continually change the packing around it. This was such a constant procedure that her abdomen was actually left open for easy access.

Later that afternoon Steph and I went over to Children's Hospital to see Aaryn, again. Though she was still very sore and bruised, her condition wasn't serious, and she was released that same day. We then went back to be with Kristy, again.

We tried to remain encouraged, and I wholeheartedly believed that God was going to perform the miracle that we were so desperately praying for. The nurse attending to Kristy told us to go home and get some rest. She promised to call if there were any changes. It was late but we stopped to see Gabe and Terryann before going home. I prayed myself to sleep that night.

Wednesday, May 4

The next morning we once again met with the doctors. They were trying to give us all the hope that they could. Kristy was now breathing less on her own. Again, that whole day we would be encouraged one moment at some little change, and the next moment discouragement would once again set in as something else would worsen. We went through this so many times that my frustrations were starting to build up. I finally told Steph that my emotions couldn't take any more of this going back and forth. I didn't want to hear any more reports. I just wanted to keep praying and trusting in God. When they were certain that Kristy was out of danger, then tell me. Until then, I didn't want to hear any more. I cannot explain how this starts to break you down after awhile, both emotionally and physically.

My faith was starting to weaken, and for the first time I feared that God just might really let my daughter die. Even though this may have been His will, I just wasn't yet ready to accept it.

Meanwhile preparations were being made for Dani's funeral. I begged them to wait just in case Kristy would somehow miraculously come out of this. I feared the thought of burying that little girl and then Kristy waking up hearing that not only had her baby died, but she had already been put in the ground. Everyone agreed to wait as long as possible.

People were constantly with us. There were very few moments that Steph and I were alone at the hospital. Not only did we have support from our own families and church body, but numerous people from other churches came to visit and pray with us as well. We had pastors and ministers from churches all around stop in and let us know that their entire congregations were holding us up in prayer. We later learned that because of all these people showing their support, Kristy was the talk of the hospital.

Pastor Tim told me that, one day while visiting, he went to the desk of a worker at the hospital to ask her something. She wasn't at her desk but noticed that she was back in a little office off to the side. She had been crying. When she noticed Pastor Tim standing there she came out and apologized. She told him that she was thinking of the girl in the trauma unit who had already lost her little girl and was now fighting for her own life. This woman also had small children, and the thought of it all just brought her to tears. Kristy's tragedy was affecting people who didn't even know her.

Thursday, May 5

The doctors were getting very concerned over Kristy's lack of improvement. Looking back I think they were trying to prepare us for the inevitable, that she just wasn't going to make it. They were finally able to get her liver to stop bleeding, but it was so badly injured it just wasn't working the way it was supposed to. The problems were now beginning to mount as her kidneys were starting to shut down as well. She could no longer breathe at all on her own and she was now on total life-support. The doctors told us they didn't know how long her heart could continue at that rate. Reality was beginning to set in. If Kristy was going to make it, there would be no doubt it would have to be an absolute miracle from the hand of God. Our faith was beginning to weaken.

Matt was released from the hospital, and that afternoon he told Gabe and Terryann about Dani. I wondered how we would possibly be able to tell them about their mommy if she didn't make it. The thought of this just tore me up inside and brought me to tears.

That night, as we lay in bed, I think Steph and I both knew that Kristy just wasn't going to pull through. As hard as it was to accept, we both knew that it was God's will to bring her home. It was a strange feeling that went through me while laying there that night. As heartbroken as I was, I could still feel the peace of God surrounding me. At that moment I didn't understand that it was God's grace working in me. Through the coming days, weeks, and months, I would become very familiar with this special touch of grace.

Friday, May 6

We received a call that morning about 5:00 am to get to the hospital as soon as possible. The doctors told us that there were no signs of improvement and that Kristy was actually getting worse. They said that she may not even make it through the day. They said there was nothing more they could do. One of the doctors even admitted that without an absolute miracle from God she had no chance at all. I just wasn't yet able to cope with the inevitable; therefore, I still wasn't ready to give up.

I had to get away from all the noise, beeping machines, and the confusion that was crowding my mind. Together, Steph and I went to the hospital chapel and prayed. I begged

God for a miracle. Then I asked Him to at least provide us the strength it was going to take to get through this if indeed it was His will to take Kristy. God's Holy Spirit entered that room as we were praying, and there was such an indescribable peace that surrounded us. Again, I cannot explain it. My heart was broken, my spirit was downtrodden, and my faith was practically nil, but I sensed the presence and peace of my loving, Heavenly Father whispering to me, "It will be all right my son, it will be all right." Grace was at work. Grace that I had never known nor experienced before.

Later that afternoon they started Kristy on dialysis as her kidneys were now completely shut down. All restrictions for visitation in the trauma room were lifted as they were letting anyone who wanted to come back and see Kristy. I think they were graciously allowing everyone to say good-bye to her even though she was still comatose.

We had a very special nurse who was with us most of the week looking after Kristy. Her name was Erin. Erin was so kind and gentle, keeping us informed at all times of what was going on, and generally just doing everything in her power to make us as comfortable as we could possibly be under the circumstances.

That night Erin came in with a pan of water, shampoo, brush, and comb and washed Kristy's hair. Actually, Erin started the procedure and let Steph complete it. I think she somehow sensed how good that would make Steph feel to be able to do this for her daughter. That's just the way Erin was. She was a very caring person and we will never forget the special attention she gave to Kristy during that entire week.

Later that evening, one of the doctors wanted to talk to me and Steph. He was very honest and told us that we needed to be thinking about making a decision of what we wanted to do if Kristy's condition didn't improve. I knew that this was a conversation that Matt needed to be involved in. Though he was released from the hospital, Matt's injuries were such that he still couldn't move around easily, so he was unable to stay with Kristy as much as he would have liked. I called Matt and told him about the conversation that Steph and I were having with the doctor. I then handed the phone to the doctor and told him to talk to my son-in-law.

The next day I went to see Matt. He told me that after talking to the doctor a peace surrounded him that night like he had never experienced before. He knew in his heart that God was wanting to bring Kristy home, and he was at peace with that. I, on the other hand was having a very difficult time accepting it. Ultimately, I knew that Matt was the one who would make the final decision, but he graciously allowed Steph and me to come to the same peace that he had experienced. I asked him to please wait a little longer, and he consented.

Saturday, May 7

There was no change in Kristy's condition, but I still couldn't bring myself to let go of her. Again, I asked for just one more day. "Please, just wait one more day," I begged. "Let's not give up, yet." I was stalling for time, praying that God was just waiting to show Himself in His absolute power.

I want to interject something here for the sake of others who may be faced with this same decision someday. I have since witnessed others who have had to make the heart-wrenching decision to let a loved one go. They struggled with the same feelings that I was going through. They felt that to give up was giving up on God. They wrestled with the thought that letting go was showing a lack of faith in God, that He was not able to heal their loved one. I went through all of those same emotions, and again, it is heart wrenching. The Lord spoke something to my heart after Kristy died that was so simple, and it helped erase the guilt of letting my precious daughter go. He said, "If I wanted to heal her, don't you think I could have done it even without the machines that were keeping her alive?" That is so true. Life-support or not, God is able to restore a person to wholeness if He so desires.

It was becoming so obvious that God wanted to bring Kristy home. I truly believe that the only reason He hadn't yet done so was because of those of us who were having such a hard time accepting it. In His wondrous mercy God was allowing us to prepare ourselves mentally, emotionally, spiritually, and physically. What a loving God we serve that He would delay His plan and His will while preparing our hearts to accept what He was going to do.

Even though Kristy was comatose, the doctors and nurses encouraged us to talk to her. I told her to please keep fighting. I was being selfish, though. I was asking her to trade in the paradise that awaited her for life here on this earth. What an unfair thing to ask. In my mind, though, all I could think was, "How can I let my baby girl go?"

Sunday, May 8 – Mothers' Day

The doctors were now waiting for us to make a decision. Were we going to allow Kristy to remain on life support, or let her go? As difficult as it was, Steph had even now accepted the fact that God wanted to bring Kristy home to be with Him and Dani. Matt came to see Kristy that morning and I looked over at him. I said, "Please, just a little while longer." Again, he consented to my selfish pleas.

Trying everything they knew to do, the doctors increased Kristy's medication as well as her heart rate. There were times when her heart rate actually reached 160-170 beats per minute, which was well beyond double the normal human heart rate. I went to the cafeteria just trying to stay moving while the medication was working in her body.

I was told that it was a somber service at the Heritage church that morning. They realized that Kristy wasn't going to make it and their hearts were breaking for us. After the service many of them came to the hospital just to be with us in our hour of need.

After about thirty minutes or so I went back to the trauma unit. Steph was standing next to Kristy, and I wasn't prepared for what I was about to see. The medicine was being pumped into Kristy's body so fast that she was swelling up all over. The fluids were running out of her eyes, ears, nose, and even the pores of her skin. I couldn't stand to see my daughter lying there like that, and I just looked at Steph and the nurse who was there and said, "Stop it. Stop it. Let her go." I looked at Matt and said to him, "We have to let her go, don't we? God wants to bring her home." He nodded at me in agreement, and they began to take her off life support.

As I looked at her I remembered something that Kristy said to me just a few weeks earlier. You may remember the Terri Schiavo case back in 1998 that lasted for seven years. Terri Schiavo collapsed in her home on February 25, 1990, and experienced respiratory and cardiac arrest, leading to fifteen years of institutionalization and a diagnosis of persistent vegetative state (PVS). In 1998 her husband petitioned the courts to remove her feeding tube, while her parents opposed and fought for her right to live. I remember Kristy saying to me, "If I am ever in a vegetative state or on life-support, please let me die. Let me go to be with the Lord." I was going against my daughter's wishes. I knew that we had to let her go.

They unhooked the machines, and about twenty minutes later at 2:30 pm Kristy went to be with Jesus, and was reunited with Dani who went to heaven just seven days earlier. How happy the two of them must have been as mother and daughter met and rejoiced in one another's arms. I have often marveled at the irony associated with Kristy's death that afternoon. My daughter wanted nothing more out of life than to be a loving mother. Her children were her life. I have to believe that God saw it fitting to bring her home to heaven on Mother's Day.

There were so many people from the church that came to the hospital that they had to open a surgical waiting room, which was normally closed on Sunday. It was almost filled to capacity as Steph and I walked into that room. We sat down and our family and dear friends then knew that she was gone. I heard no one talking. There was just a hush that filled the room and quiet crying as everyone in their own way was trying to come to grips with what had just taken place.

When Steph and I got home that night, I pulled into my driveway and parked the car. Before going inside I glanced down at the empty house where my daughter and grand-daughter would never be coming back to. I thought of how, in an instant, one's life can change. I would soon learn that what I once considered a blessing—to live just two doors away from my daughter, son-in-law, and grandchildren—would quickly become a great pain for us to bear. Though Steph and I were happy to live close by to help Matt and the other three grandkids in any way that we could, the constant reminder of what used to be was heartbreaking at times.

As I continued to peer into their front yard, I became broken by the thought that I would never see them walking down the sidewalk to our house again. I would never hear their laughter again as they played outside on a warm and sunny day. I cried myself to sleep that night.

Thursday, May 12

Kristy and Dani's funerals were together. I know that is the way Kristy would have wanted it. I remember sitting there and thinking how I never thought I would ever be attending my own daughter's funeral. So much of that day was just a blur. I remember there was beautiful singing, and Pastor Tim preached a wonderful message. The church was filled to capacity, and people had to stand out in the foyer area.

I have already talked about how supportive our church family was to us during this most difficult time. I want to share something which illustrates the love exhibited by this body of God's people.

My brother Danny told me that Kristy and Dani's deaths affected many of his co-workers, even though they didn't know Kristy or Dani. Because they worked with my brother, the story of the accident in the Columbus Dispatch had made an impression on them. Several of his co-workers even came to the funeral. They stood out in the foyer during the service. One of the ladies that worked with Danny said something that touched me immensely. After the service had ended the funeral director first dismissed all of the family. Then everyone else was dismissed one row at a time. This lady said she noticed the tears and sadness of each person as they passed by her. In fact, she said, "It was hard to see where the family ended and the rest of the congregation began." When Danny told me this, I thought that was a great compliment to the closeness of the people that I worshipped with at my church. That is what the body of Christ is all about. The apostle Paul called it *"bearing one another's burdens."*

I have learned since Kristy and Dani's deaths that grace often involves God using other people to reach out to the one that needs that special gift. The people at Heritage Free Will Baptist Church were certainly instruments of God's grace during this most difficult time in my life. I will always be grateful to them for their love and support.

Chapter 7

Where Are You Lord?
Part 1

And he was in the hinder part of the ship, asleep on
a pillow; and they awake him, and say unto him,
Master, carest thou not that we perish?
(Mark 4:38)

In chapter 4 of the Gospel of Mark, we read that one day
after teaching a great multitude of people, Jesus and His
disciples got into their boat and went a little ways out into
the sea. He wanted a time of rest because he was tired. He
went to sleep, and the next thing we read is that there arose a
great storm and the waves were beating into the boat.

The disciples reacted the same way most of us would
have. Even though their Master was in the boat with them,
they thought that, because He was asleep, He wasn't aware
of what was going on around them. They thought they were
surely going to drown. They even woke Jesus up and said to
Him, "*Master, carest not that we perish?*"

The Scriptures teach us that Jesus arose, rebuked the
wind, and said unto the sea, "*Peace, be still,*" and the wind
ceased and there was a great calm.

What a wonderful lesson Mark teaches us here concerning the sovereignty of God. There is much to learn here from these passages about our Savior. When we are in the storms, He is in the boat with us. When we call upon Him, He will come to our rescue, and when we open our hearts to Him with our concerns, He will meet our needs.

Another lesson we learn here is that God puts us into the storms of life in order that we might grow closer to Him and that we might know Him better.

> *Jesus, Savior, pilot me*
> *Over life's tempestuous sea;*
> *Unknown waves before me roll,*
> *Hiding rocks and treacherous shoal;*
> *Chart and compass come from Thee-*
> *Jesus, Savior, pilot me!*
> *"Jesus, Savior, Pilot Me"*
> (written by Edward Hopper,
> trad. Christian hymn)

I am led to believe that every Christian has at least one time in their life come to a point where they feel like the Lord has abandoned them. I'm talking about a particular time, situation, or circumstance where you absolutely feel all alone. You have always been taught that God will never leave you nor forsake you, and in your heart you know that He is aware of your present problem. But at that particular moment you are having difficulty believing that He really does care. As you are struggling through that storm there comes a point where you find yourself crying out, "Where are you Lord? I thought you said you would go with me all the way? I need you, but you are nowhere to be found! I just don't understand."

I have been there, my friend. At some point in your walk with God you probably have as well. We don't like to admit those times though because it's an admission of a lack of faith on our part. Isn't that why God reached down for us in the first place, though? He had to do what we were unable to do for ourselves.

As Christians, it's important to understand that God knows all about us. He knows all of our fears, shortcomings, failures, weaknesses, and inadequacies. There is absolutely nothing that we go through that He isn't aware of. Likewise, He also knows every thought that we are thinking, so He understands when our faith has weakened. During those times in our lives our Heavenly Father is not standing over us ready to scold us for not trusting Him. Rather, He is patiently waiting for us to come to Him with an open and honest heart, asking for His help that only He can give.

No one is an exception to the working power of God's grace. In other words, God will not do for me what He won't also do for you. What are you struggling with, my friend? What storm of life are you going through that makes you doubt that God is there or that He really cares? His grace reached down and touched me, and His healing grace is still at work in this unfinished vessel. I rest assured in this wonderful promise found in Philippians 1:6, *"He which hath begun a good work in you will perform it until the day of Jesus Christ."* The Lord Jesus Christ is the One who saved me. He will see me through all the way to the end, even with all of my doubts, fears, and failures. His impartial grace will do the same for you my friend.

In telling my story I want to clarify that for the most part I am only sharing my own personal feelings of what I went through in dealing with Kristy and Dani's deaths. Though Steph and I went through this horrific ordeal together, I have come to learn that everyone still deals with their own grief in their own way. For that reason God distributes His grace to each individual in a way that only He can do. In other words, there were times and moments when God had to deal with me differently than He did with Steph. While going through our own personal Gethsemane, so to speak, He had to meet us at our individual point of need. Everyone goes through tests and trials differently. Only God knows how to meet each one's need as it arises.

The Garden of Gethsemane was where Jesus went to pray right before His crucifixion (Matthew 26:36-46). He asked His disciples to pray with Him, but they fell asleep and left Him alone. Though our Savior willingly gave His life for you and me, we must never forget that He was still human. He understood that His death would be excruciatingly painful. At this intense moment of His life He was absolutely alone. During His time at Gethsemane Christ learned submission to its fullest degree. He realized that His life wasn't about self, but rather it was about being obedient to the Father and performing His will.

Likewise, we too meet with our Heavenly Father in our own unique way during times of personal crisis. It is an opportunity to gain a more intimate relationship with God if we will only trust Him as Jesus did. Though our spiritual Gethsemanes can be grueling and agonizing, they provide an opportunity for spiritual growth like we could have never known before.

What I have to share with you is meant to bring encouragement and hope where there seems to be no hope. I want you to know that there is light at the end of the proverbial tunnel if we will just continue to trust in God. Please believe me when I say that I know this is easier said than done. We serve a patient God who promised that He would never leave us nor forsake us (Hebrews 13:5). He spends a whole lot of time waiting for us to catch up with Him. One of the verses of Scripture that God spoke to my heart, from which I benefited greatly, is Psalm 46:10, *"Be still and know that I am*

God." When we give God a chance to bring us the touch, deliverance, or healing that we are so desperately in need of He will faithfully deliver. That is a guaranteed promise.

I may not be the perfect pattern to follow for the crisis you might be presently going through, but I do want you to know that God will see you through by His amazing grace. He brought healing to my broken heart when I didn't believe it to ever be possible again. When I was ready to give up on myself, my Heavenly Father never gave up on me. I am so thankful that I can say I know Him more intimately now than at any other time in my Christian life. It has not been an easy road to travel but it has been a road that has led to many rewarding victories as I have allowed Him to do a work in me that I was incapable of doing myself.

I am going to be blatantly honest with my feelings. I cannot say that I have always been proud of the way I have responded at certain times. It is my hope though that my honesty will speak to someone's heart who may be going through a similar circumstance or trial in their own life.

Everyone may react differently even though their situation or particular struggle may be similar. Everyone may go through the numerous stages of grief differently. We all deal with adversity in our own unique way, but there is one very important fact you need to understand. Regardless of how we deal with our own personal Gethsemane, every test and trial we go through requires God's grace in order to endure successfully and victoriously.

It has been over two years since the accident that took Kristy and Dani's lives. God has brought me a long way. It hasn't been without its struggles. I believe that I have experienced every emotion known to humanity. In His patience and infinite wisdom, God uses every emotion that we go through as a means to our healing. Emotions release the intentions of our heart, and it is in the heart of man that healing must begin.

If you have ever gone through a personal crisis that literally turned your world upside down, you no doubt understand the feeling of hopelessness that can overtake you. Though each person's story may be uniquely different, the emotions that we experience can be easily identified and understood by someone else who is going through their Gethsemane. I sincerely pray that my experience of how God brought me through the darkest hours of my life will somehow be of help to someone else.

I have learned more about grace since the death of my daughter and granddaughter than all the previous years of my Christian life combined. The healing process that has taken place in my life has been a result of God's grace.

A while back I was seeking God for an answer to a particular problem I was facing. The Holy Spirit directed me to the third chapter of Habakkuk. Habakkuk was a prophet to whom we can relate in our present time. He struggled with the question of the ages: "why does God allow bad things to happen?" Habakkuk lived in a time of great national corruption: when crime, hatred, and division were on the rise, when evil and immorality were not shameful to be openly flaunted, and when ethical standards and family values were unheard of. Honestly, Habakkuk could not have been any more discouraged at the conditions in which he lived. Through it all, though, he learned that, in the bleakest of times, the grace, mercy, and love of God shines through.

We can learn much from Habakkuk if we will adopt his attitude into our lives during the tough times. I want you to read closely the words of this great man of God found in Habakkuk 3:17-19. "*Although the fig tree shall not blossom, neither shall fruit be in the vines; the labour of the olive tree shall fail, and the fields shall yield no meat; the flock shall* be cut off from the fold, and there shall be no herd in the stalls..." (verse 17).

Now it really doesn't sound like there is too much to rejoice about here, does it? Putting this verse in terms we can more easily understand, Habakkuk was saying, "Absolutely nothing is going right for me. Everything in which I become involved falls apart. Everything I touch breaks. How much worse could it get?"

Read on, though, at how this servant of God responded when things seemed like they could get no worse. *"Yet I will rejoice in the Lord, I will joy in the God of my salvation. The Lord God is my strength, and he will make my feet like hinds' feet, and he will make me to walk upon high places"* (verses 18, 19).

Habakkuk realized that his hope was not in the things of this world. His hope and trust were in the Lord God Almighty. He refused to allow circumstances to dictate his life; rather, he allowed God to control his circumstances. If we can learn to trust in God as Habakkuk did then we will be able to overcome any situation, circumstance, or obstacle that comes our way. We, too, will rejoice in the Lord, for we will know He is our strength.

****

So many people reached out to my family during this time of crisis in our lives. I'm not just talking about other Christians and immediate family who were there for us. It was amazing at how friends, co-workers, and neighbors reached out to us as well. God knows just what we need and when we need it. He really is an on-time God. As I journey through the two-plus years since Kristy and Dani's deaths you will see how so many people played such an integral part in helping us during our healing process. I believe you will also get a real sense of the tremendous spiritual warfare that we faced on a daily basis.

I mentioned earlier that I am not proud of the way I responded at times when facing the onslaught of the enemy. I must be honest and say there were times when I just felt like giving up. I hope my honesty will encourage someone else who may be struggling, who may have also said, "I blew it; God can no longer use me." That is simply not true. God is not waiting to scold you for failing. He is patiently waiting on you to succumb to His will for your life. He has never left you nor forsaken you. He has never lifted His hand from you nor taken His eyes off of you. He loves you, and He wants to heal your broken heart... if you will let Him.

Throughout my story, you see the emotional roller coaster ride that has taken place in mine and Steph's lives. Another one of the many amazing things I have learned about my God: regardless of what transpires in my life, He can use it for my good if I will let Him. Yes, I know that is a truth that we have all heard and believed. Romans 8:28 does tell us *"that all things work together for good to them that love God, to them who are the called according to his purpose."* I have become a firm believer, though, that we cannot really understand the impact of that promise until we have experienced it firsthand. It is through and by these precious promises over the past several months that I have grown in God's grace and knowledge. It is through learning to trust in Him when I've had no where else to turn that I have become more intimate with Jesus Christ, my Lord and Savior. He has made Himself more real to me than I could have ever imagined, and I thank Him for it. Through it all I can say without any doubt or wavering in my heart that my God has never let me down. I may not have complete understanding on all things, but He has assured me that He is sovereign and nothing happens to one of His children unless He allows it. What a comforting thought that is.

May 13, 2005 (one day after Kristy and Dani were buried)

I was off work for the next five weeks. I just needed time to get my thoughts together. It all seemed so hard to believe. Only thirteen days earlier, Steph and I were having lunch after church with our daughter and her family, and now she was buried. Needless to say, reality hadn't really, yet, begun to sink in.

I talked about people reaching out to us whom we wouldn't have expected. My work is a perfect example. I had just started a new job only eight months earlier, so I hadn't been there long enough to accumulate any significant sick time. Several co-workers stepped forward and offered me their own sick days so that I could take off work as long as I needed. I will be forever grateful to Carla who gave me enough of her own personal time to allow me to be off for five weeks. Again, I say, God uses people.

Steph was off work for four months. She just wasn't yet mentally prepared to return. Her employer was so kind to her in giving her whatever she needed, as well as numerous other co-workers who reached out in a variety of ways. The generosity of so many kind people will never be forgotten.

In the months following Kristy's death, my first emotion was one of numbness. As real as the pain of this terrible tragedy was, there was a part of me that was oblivious to all that was going on around me. Maybe it was denial of wanting to accept the truth; maybe it was what I refer to as functional shock. By functional shock I mean that your natural body continues to function according to its normal daily activities, but the inner man or spirit man (that part of us that is entangled in spiritual warfare) doesn't seem to be able to think and react clearly. This especially becomes true concerning spiritual issues because the enemy of our soul (Satan) is standing close by ready to destroy you with his lies and deception. This would ultimately become my greatest battle.

After the death of a loved one it's not uncommon to be surrounded at first by many friends and loved ones. This constant act of support helps delay reality from setting in like it eventually will. As cruel as it may sound to the one who feels like they have just lost everything, life really must go on. People slowly start going back to their normal routines, and one day you find yourself alone with your thoughts in a way that you hadn't yet experienced. The reality that your departed loved one will never be able to call you again, go out to lunch with you, visit you, or take trips with you starts to set in as it hadn't before. All of those emotions which were bottled up inside of you that you thought you had a grip on suddenly start coming to the surface. Before long the numbness is replaced by loneliness, depression, fear, despondency, guilt, anger, bitterness, hostility, or any other number of emotions known to man. Many times it is a vicious cycle that must run its course. The emotions can become so intense that it literally affects our relationships, not only with just those around us, but with God as well.

Don't ever underestimate the importance of reaching out to someone who may be grieving over the loss of a loved one. A card, short note, phone call, or a drop-by visit to simply say "I just wanted you to know that I was thinking about you," is oftentimes the exact medication that person needed So, when you feel the urge to do any of those things, be assured that it is most likely the Holy Spirit speaking to your heart to reach out to someone who is desperately in need. You will be rewarded for being obedient, and someone in need will be blessed. This is just one of the many ways in which our God uses us.

That first month after Kristy and Dani's deaths, Steph and I spent a lot of evenings over at Pastor Tim and Tobianne's house. They opened their home to us and allowed us to just share our hearts with them. I always appreciated the way Pastor Tim would just allow us to talk while he and Tobianne listened. He was very honest with me and even said, "Terry, I just don't know what to say but I am always willing to sit and listen as you share your heart with me." What Tim didn't realize was that was the best thing he could have done. Honestly, there was nothing he could have said at that time to take the pain away. We just needed someone to spend time with.

If you know someone who is going through the grieving process, let me give you the best advice I can think of to be of help to them. As my pastor was willing to listen to us, do the same for that person who is grieving. So often we think that we have to come up with some great theological answer from God's Word to make sense of what has happened that has brought such pain to our lives. That's the farthest thing from the truth though. Again, the only two things anyone ever said to me that made any sense at that time was, "I'm praying for you," or, "I just don't know what to say." Nothing else even came remotely close to registering in my mind. What I needed most was someone to lean on and listen to my burdened heart.

There were so many people in our church who were instrumental in helping us cope and move on with our lives. It really wouldn't be fair to start naming names because there were so many that reached out to us in numerous ways. I'm sure that most of them didn't realize it, but each time they did something special it was usually at a time when we needed it the most.

There is one couple God sent our way that I have to mention though. Jim and Paula Fraley became dear and precious friends to Steph and me. For the longest time there wasn't a day that went by that they didn't call or stop in to see how we were doing. We became almost inseparable over the next several months and there has been a bond created between the four of us that I don't believe will ever be broken. Through our relationship with Jim and Paula, we have grown close to their children as well. Their three daughters loved Kristy immensely and her death touched them deeply.

Some of our best times with Jim and Paula have been spent at the Amish country for a weekend get away. I will never forget the first time we went there together. I think it was the first time I really saw Steph laugh since Kristy died. Those times that we got away with Jim and Paula were spiritually therapeutic to our burdened hearts.

Jim and Paula were gifted listeners. They also seemed to always know just the right thing to say and when to say it. God truly sent them our way at just the right time. Our dear friends would shed tears with us as we talked about those things that needed to be released from our troubled hearts. Even during my most troubling moments, when bitterness seized hold of me, Jim never condemned me. He listened and allowed me to talk and would then follow up with words of encouragement to lift my troubled spirit.

Something else that I always appreciate about Jim and Paula was the way they were so open to talk about Kristy and Dani with us. Though they are no longer with us in this life, Kristy and Dani are still alive, and they certainly will never be forgotten. In fact, I have told many people they are more alive than we are. Unless the Lord returns, each of us still has to face death. Kristy and Dani have already conquered that foe. Jim and Paula were so comfortable in talking about them with us, and I always appreciated that.

Over the course of time I discovered that so many people were afraid to talk about Kristy and Dani with us. Maybe we are exceptions (I don't think so though), but we love keeping the memories of our daughter and granddaughter alive by talking about them. I believe that some people think that by talking about them they are continually bringing up painful memories. May I say this though: whether I am talking about Kristy or not, she and Dani are always on my mind. It is a scar that will never go away. The pain may ease but the scar will remain forever. I believe talking about our departed loved ones is an integral part of the healing process. Steph and I continually talk about Kristy to our grandkids. We never want them to forget her. Even Aaryn, who was only eight months old when her mommy died, now talks about Mommy Kristy and asks to listen to her mommy sing on the CD we have of her. Steph and I always want people to feel comfortable in talking about Kristy and Dani with us. Don't be afraid to ask the grieving person if they would care to talk about their loved one who has gone on. I think you will find they usually do to.

It really became overwhelming to my mental state at how one day to the next could bring such a change in the way I felt. One day I would think that things were starting to seem better and the next day I felt as though I just couldn't go on.

There are many stages to the healing process and each stage seems to bring on new battles, both mentally and spiritually. Emotions wear the body down. Think about it; even too much laughter can make the body tired after a while. So, imagine what depression, loneliness, guilt, hostility, anger, and bitterness can do to the weary and downtrodden heart of a person. When the body wears down, Satan is standing close by ready to attack the mind, which is where the battle-field lies. *The grieving or hurting individual becomes vulnerable to the deceit, lies, and vicious onslaught of the devil.* Please keep that thought in mind as I talk about my own experience.

My grieving heart allowed Satan to rob me of my peace and joy in serving God. The things that I once dearly loved doing were becoming a chore for me. I always enjoyed teaching and preaching. I was beginning to discover though that I no longer enjoyed doing either. My thought process was chaotic to say the least and it was a struggle just putting a lesson together. I felt hypocritical as I stood in front of my class teaching them from God's Word, when quite honestly I was struggling in my personal prayer and study life. I may have appeared all right on the outside, but on the inside I felt as though I was being ripped apart.

We often talk about how God and Satan are as opposite as the mind can imagine. God is love and truth, while Satan is full of hate and lies. Our Heavenly Father is merciful and full of grace, while Satan is condemning and always reminding us of our past. God is a restorer, and Satan is a destroyer. God is light, and Satan is darkness. The parallels that separate the goodness of God and the evilness of Satan are innumerable, but I have always claimed there is one thing they have in common. Acts 10:34 says that *"God is not a respector of persons."* I would like to go on record as saying neither is Satan. Of course, though, even that truth of neither one respecting any one person more than another is found to be at opposite ends of the spectrum as well. God shows no respect (or favoritism) of His creation, in that Jesus Christ died for each and every person ever created so they may have the opportunity to attain eternal life. Satan shows no favoritism to God's creation in that it is his desire to lead everyone that he can away from the truth.

You have heard the saying, "Don't kick someone while they are down." Satan certainly doesn't live according to that policy. In fact, that is when he really starts going to work. When someone is at their weakest, he wastes no time in pouncing upon them.

I was becoming weak and tired from the daily struggles. Slowly my hurt and grief began to turn into anger and bitterness. I tried hard not to admit it, but most of my anger was directed toward God. After all, wasn't He the One who allowed my daughter and granddaughter to die? He could have prevented it if He wanted to. He knew how much this was going to hurt me. Didn't He care? How could He really expect me to continue to minister for Him after He just ripped my heart out?

Satan was having a wonderful and successful time lying to me. In my weakened condition I was beginning to believe every lie he was whispering to me. I was now hearing him speak to me more clearly than I could hear the tender and loving voice of the Holy Spirit. How was I ever going to get past this horrific pain and hurt?

Meanwhile, things weren't going very well at home either. Satan was wanting to destroy my marriage as well. Steph and I were both going through our own individual struggles and it was taking its toll on our relationship. The most important part of any marriage is constant communication with one another. Our communication had practically come to a halt. There were days and nights when we just sat together in absolute silence. It wasn't because we were angry at one another. It was because the grief we bore was so great that we were totally absorbed only in our own individual pain. I believe Steph and I were slowly growing apart and didn't even realize it.

I was ready to give up on my ministry. It didn't seem like it even mattered to me anymore. For the longest time the only thing that kept me from handing in my ordination credentials was that I knew Kristy would be disappointed in me. My whole focus was entirely wrong. I was more interested in pleasing my daughter who was now gone than I was in pleasing the Lord. I knew this wasn't right, but I just couldn't get past it. I know that it was the prayers of many people that carried me through each day when I didn't think I could survive one more day.

> *Never underestimate the power of prayer. So many times we think there is nothing we can do to help someone who is hurting. To the child of God, prayer is our greatest asset. It's not uncommon for the hurting person to become totally defenseless in their spiritual life. It's during these times that brothers and sisters in Christ need to pick up the spiritual slack and be ready to carry heavy burdens as described by the apostle Paul in Galatians 6:2. I thank God that many loving members in the body of Christ carried me through by the power of prayer. I have learned a very valuable lesson through my trials: "yes, we are our brother's keeper."*

Chapter 8

Where Are You Lord?
Part 2

And he arose, and rebuked the wind, and saith unto
the sea, Peace, be still. And the wind ceased, and
there was a great calm.
(Mark 4:39)

I want you to know that there was never a point in time where God's grace wasn't there carrying us through. Looking back, I now see a much clearer picture of how grace was at work in my life the whole time. There are two important things to realize concerning grace. The first one is that God's grace is always there for the one who is so desperately in need of it. The second truth and the one that we most often struggle with is that God will not force His grace upon us. It is freely given and it must be accepted with a humble heart. His grace is never wasted. God always gives us exactly what we need when we need it.

Kristy and Dani had been gone for almost seven months as the holidays approached. I cannot tell you how much I dreaded going through the holidays without our daughter and granddaughter. Steph and I both wished that we could just go away somewhere.

It was Thanksgiving Day 2005. We were to go over to each of our parents' homes later in the day. I will never forget how lonely I felt that day wishing that Kristy and Dani were with us. I was up very early that morning, and I told Steph that I really didn't want to go anywhere. I just wanted to stay home. We sat in the living room together for a while with our conversation at a minimum. That was a routine to which we were becoming accustomed. After a while I decided to go back to bed.

I had fallen off to sleep. I hadn't been asleep for very long when I woke up. I don't know if you would call it a vision, or a trance, but I do know that I wasn't dreaming. I didn't know where I was, but I do remember that I had been crying. I was thinking about Gabe and Terryann. My heart was burdened for them because their mommy wasn't going to be with them this day, or for Christmas which was just around the corner. I was leaning up against a wall with my head down and resting against my right arm. Suddenly I felt a touch on my shoulder. I turned around and there stood Kristy smiling at me. She looked so beautiful, and she was exactly as I knew her here. She had a glow all around her. Not only could I see the peace, happiness, and the joy of the Lord that was upon her, I could feel it as well. I was speechless. I wanted to speak to her but I knew that I was supposed to listen. I knew that she had a message for me. Still smiling, she spoke softly to me, "Dad, don't worry. Gabe and Terryann will be all right. They love you and mom and they will be all right. Dad, I love you and mom. Dani loves you and mom, and we are all right too." She then stepped toward me and gave me a hug. It wasn't like a hug of goodbye, but rather a hug that said, "I love you and I will see you again in a little while." The next thing I knew I was lying there in bed, eyes wide open, realizing that God had just allowed me to see my daughter in a way that only He could. My Heavenly Father knew exactly what I needed that morning and He provided me with it. I will never forget those precious moments that I experienced that Thanksgiving morning.

I realize that some are skeptical and believe God would not really allow something such as this to happen. They dismiss it as a dream or an active imagination that wants something so badly that the mind caused it to happen. Though I do care what others may think, I cannot doubt what I know God allowed me to experience that Thanksgiving morning. I know that His grace goes far beyond the understanding of any mortal man. I also believe that His grace works in many different ways. God knows what each one of us needs, and He knows precisely when we need it. He is not limited or bound to anything that He chooses to accomplish, other than His own Word.

When one loses a child, there is no such thing as getting over it. I have often used the analogy of losing an arm or a leg. Though your life has not ended and you learn to go on without that essential part of your body, there is never a moment that you are not aware that the limb is missing. The wound may heal, but the scar will remain forever.

It's the same with the loss of a child. God's grace gives you the ability to go on and cope with life but there is never a moment, not even one second that you don't realize that they are no longer with you. Kristy is the last thing on my mind when I fall asleep each night and she is the first thing on my mind when I wake up the next morning. In fact, until God allowed me to see her that Thanksgiving morning, there was hardly a night prior to that that I never dreamed about her. Since that morning, though, I probably could count on just one hand how many times I have dreamed about her. God gave me a peace that morning that allowed me to rest in such a way that I was unable to before. His grace never stops working.

As the months went by, I still continued to struggle. I missed Kristy and Dani so much and just couldn't seem to get past many of the things that were tormenting me. As I think back, it is now so clear how Satan was out to destroy me, my marriage, and my ministry. I was weakening under the intense pressure, and even my pastor and dearest friends could only provide temporary relief. When I was at home or all alone, Satan's voice constantly echoed in my ear. I was fighting depression while trying to put on a façade that I was doing fine. Only those who were closest to me understood the daily battles that I was facing, and quite honestly I tried to fool them as best as I could. I thought that was what I was supposed to do. I have to confess that there were times when I was bitter and angry at God but was afraid to voice it aloud. Oh, I had my moments where I cried out to God in anger, but I was afraid to tell Him how I really felt, and that was a mistake on my part. It's silly to think that if we don't speak it aloud we cannot be held accountable for the thoughts that are in our heart. God knows our thoughts as well as the words we speak aloud. He wants us to be honest with Him. In fact, honesty with our Heavenly Father is an important step in our healing process.

I cannot stress this enough to the person who feels hurt or betrayed by God. Be honest with God. Don't be afraid to tell Him how you feel. He knows what you are thinking anyway! God wants you to be open with Him in all of your thoughts and feelings. When we come to this point, we are on the right road to recovery. No healing is possible without honesty. It was honesty with God that you were a sinner in need of His forgiveness that opened the door to your eternal salvation. Doesn't it stand to reason that honesty with the One who loved you enough to give His very life for you is essential to every part of your life that you have now surrendered to Him? When I finally came to God in sincere honesty, I felt a huge burden fall from my shoulders. I knew the areas of my life where I needed help, and I discovered that my Heavenly Father wasn't there waiting to scold me. On the contrary, He was standing there with arms open wide asking me to trust Him. Admittedly, it took me a long time to come to that place. Being honest with God in how you really feel is one of the first suggestions I would offer to any person who feels betrayed by their Savior.

Before I came to this essential point in my life I was continuing to struggle in every facet of my life. I wanted to leave the ministry. I was being tormented by the fact that my desire to minister was no longer there, and now I was also plagued by the lies of Satan that I was unworthy to call myself a servant of God. I never stopped to consider that there never was a time when I was worthy to begin with. I was being bombarded by his lies and deceit and it wouldn't be long before it reached its boiling point.

I want you to understand that even when I was being hit hardest by the onslaught of Satan, God's grace was still at work. He sustained me even when I wasn't aware of it. Often times He used people to get me through one more day. That was because I wasn't spiritually able to hear Him myself. The lies of Satan will destroy your thinking. What is right suddenly seems wrong, and what is wrong appears to be right. It is a dangerous and vulnerable state to be in, and that is exactly where I was at.

It was now early-to-mid-February 2006. I felt like I had reached my end. Satan wouldn't let up. Steph was still struggling immensely and I felt helpless in my ability as a husband to provide the help that she needed. He (Satan) convinced me that I was being a hypocrite to my church family by acting like I was all right when I really felt miserable and useless to God. He told me that I was lying to my Sunday School class every time I taught about how loving God was, when all the while I believed He had hurt me and didn't care. Satan's lies succeeded in making me believe that I was being deceitful to God and my church every time I preached His Word.

Though I never heard an audible voice speaking to me, I recognized that it was the devil himself speaking to my heart. I reached the place where I was actually talking back to him aloud just as I prayed aloud to God. I begged him to leave me alone, and I was ready to even make a deal with him. I don't say this proudly. I only want you to see how far he had gotten into my head.

What I said to Satan next may sound almost blasphemous, but I hope you understand the weak spiritual condition I was now in. Again, I begged him to leave me alone. I was ready to deal with him. I told Satan that I would give up my ministry, and I would even leave my church that I loved so dearly, if he would just let up on me. I could no longer stand against his piercing accusations. I just needed relief. I told him that my deal did not include turning my back on God to the point of denying my salvation, though, because I knew that was the only way I would ever see my daughter and granddaughter again. I'm sure you are beginning to understand just how far off-base I had gotten spiritually. God was patiently waiting for me to talk with Him instead of my enemy.

That following Sunday morning I went to the altar and prayed. Church dismissed but I felt the need to just stay and pray. Pastor Tim and several brothers stayed and prayed with me. I shared with them all the thoughts that had been running through my mind and that it might be best if I just left the church. If Job would have had friends like my family at the Heritage Free Will Baptist church then his ordeal would not have been nearly as tough to go through. My church family was always so supportive. No one ever pretended to understand the pain Steph and I were experiencing. Nor did anyone ever try to give us reasons or senseless explanations to the many questions that were in our minds. They patiently stood by us, befriended us, and allowed God to bring us the healing we were so much in need of. I have often said that the people at Heritage Free Will Baptist Church are the epitome of what Christianity is all about.

After praying that morning I did feel much better, but I knew that there were still things that I never left at the altar. I opened up to my brothers how the devil was attacking my mind. I still needed to be honest with God though. He was the One that I needed to come to in sincerity and truth.

I have learned that what God desires more than anything else from you and me is intimate fellowship. He wants us to come to Him and pour our hearts out to Him. God craves our fellowship because He loves us so much. Sometimes He even allows things to come against us, knowing that it will ultimately be the thing that causes us to come back to Him.

Do you remember how God placed restrictions on Satan against Job? God knew Job's breaking point, and Satan was not permitted to cross that line. God also knew my breaking point. He only allowed Satan to torment me to a certain point, and then he had to back off. As hard as this may be for some people to understand, it was God's love that allowed Satan to torment me until I just wanted to give up. You may be thinking, "That doesn't make sense, Terry. Hadn't you already been through enough in losing your daughter and granddaughter? Wasn't God really being unfair to you now by allowing Satan to tear down the small remainder of what was left of you?" No, my Heavenly Father wasn't being unfair or mean to me. He was using the very thing that He knew would ultimately bring me back to Him. For months God desired the intimate fellowship that He and I once experienced together. In His loving and omniscient way He knew exactly how to bring me back to Him. He was about to show me that our new relationship would be greater than anything I had ever known before.

A few days later I went back to the altar. I was there alone, just me and God, and at last I was ready to open my heart to my Heavenly Father. Do you know what I discovered? He was there waiting on me. Not once did He condemn me for not coming sooner. He never scolded me or told me that I was no longer any use to Him in the ministry. He never attacked me with accusations by saying I had crossed His line of forgiveness. Nor did my Heavenly Father even question all of my false accusations against His right to do as He pleases because He is God. What I discovered was that He had been waiting on me to come to Him. He was happy to see me and now He only wanted to have fellowship with me.

I knelt down before God on bended knees and suddenly my heart melted before Him.

Did you know that when you are in the presence of God audible words need not be spoken? Our broken hearts before an omniscient God speak louder than words. He knows why we are there before Him, and He is ready with a touch from above that only He can supply.

I started my prayer not knowing exactly what to say. Soon, though, I felt the presence of God like I had not felt for several months. It felt so good just basking in His presence and feeling His touch. Romans 8:26 tells us, "*Likewise the Spirit also helpeth our infirmities: for we know not what we should pray for as we ought: but the Spirit itself maketh intercession for us with groanings which cannot be uttered.*" That is exactly what the Holy Spirit did for me that day at the altar. I didn't even know where to start in my conversation with the Lord, but the Holy Spirit started my prayer for me. With His leading it wasn't long before the words poured freely from my own lips unto my Savior.

I soon learned that I had nothing to dread or fear. God was asking me to be open and honest with Him. He wanted me to share all of my fears, inhibitions, bitterness, anger, accusations against Him, and anything else that was troubling me. He was asking me to hold nothing back, because when I gave it to Him I would no longer be holding on to it myself. I had to let go of everything that was troubling me before I could lay it down on that altar though.

So often we make claims that we have laid something down at the altar when in reality we never let go of it at all. In order to truly lay something down we have to be willing to open our arms and hearts before God and say to Him, "Please take it Lord, this thing is a snare unto me. It is the root of the problem that is keeping me from drawing closer to you." When we come before God in an attitude of humility and repentance, He will always meet you at your point of need. When you lay it down, though, release it from your grasp, extend your hands and arms toward heaven, and "LEAVE IT THERE!"

That day at the altar I opened my heart before the Lord as I hadn't done in months. I did exactly as He asked me to do. I told God that I had been angry with Him. I cried out to Him that I didn't understand why he was allowing me to hurt so much. "Why, oh, Lord?" I prayed. "Why did you take Kristy and Dani when you knew how much it would hurt me?"

It was a strange sensation that came over me as I opened my heart to the Lord. I was telling Him things that I had previously been afraid to say aloud. The Holy Spirit brought a peace and calmness to me that assured me this was what God wanted from me. I continued to tell the Lord that I was angry at Him for what he had allowed to happen. As ridiculous as it may sound I wanted to get back at God. The only way that I knew to get back at Him was by refusing to do the things He had called me to do.

I told God that I never wanted to teach or preach His Word again. I don't know how long I knelt there in prayer, but I held absolutely nothing back. As I continued praying, there came a moment when my heart totally broke before the Lord. Suddenly, my bitterness toward God turned into repentance. As I prayed, He touched me in a way that I wouldn't allow Him to before.

I had closed God out and refused the help that He wanted to give me. Though He never left me nor forsook me at any time, still I would not grant Him permission to give me the touch that I so desperately needed.

God's grace and mercy are unlimited, and He supplies them to us even when we don't realize it. I have often used the poem "Footprints in the Sand" by Mary Stevenson to explain how I've felt these past few years. I'm sure most of you are familiar with this wonderful poem. No doubt, there have been instances in your life when you have been able to relate to its truths. I believe it to be worth repeating.

Footprints in the Sand

One night a man had a dream. He dreamed he was walking along the beach with the Lord. Across the sky flashed scenes from his life. For each scene, he noticed two sets of footprints in the sand: one belonging to him, and the other to the Lord. When the last scene of his life flashed before him, he looked back at the footprints in the sand. He noticed that many times along the path of his life there was only one set of footprints. He also noticed that it happened at the very lowest and saddest times in his life. This really bothered him and he questioned the Lord about it. "Lord, You said that once I decided to follow you, You'd walk with me all the way. But I have noticed that during the most troublesome times in my life, there is only one set of footprints. I don't understand why when I needed you most you would leave me." The Lord replied, "My son, My precious child, I love you and I would never leave you. During your times of trial and suffering, when you see only one set of footprints, it was then that I carried you."

I can relate well to this story. Many times during these past few years God has carried me. When I thought He had abandoned me, He was actually sheltering me and protecting me in ways that I never knew or understood.

The complexity of an omniscient, omnipotent, and omnipresent God as compared to human mortality causes us to fall short in understanding His grace to its fullest potential. Though He will never leave us nor forsake us, He will not force His grace upon us. Just as He doesn't force salvation by grace upon anyone, God will not force healing grace upon us. We have to be willing to accept it. Just as it takes some people years to finally accept the grace of salvation, it sometimes takes just as long to accept His healing grace. It had almost been ten months since Kristy died and I was just now beginning to accept the healing that the Lord wanted to bestow upon me. God's grace is also patient.

I got up from praying, and knew that I had been in the presence of God. I felt His touch, and I had a change in my heart. Though I would still face new battles in the months to come, God had touched me, and I was now consciously aware of His grace that was at work in my life. I knew He had not given up on me, and for the first time in months I felt like He could still use me in the ministry. I felt like I had been born-again all over.

The devil has never given up on spreading his lies and deception. He still tries to discourage me, and there are days when I feel like he has gotten the best of me. Ever since that day, though, when I laid myself on the altar and got honest before God, I have been able to fight Satan off. I know that the battle is not mine, it is the Lord's, and He graciously fights for me. When I go to the Word or call upon Jesus Christ, the devil has to flee. If I would have done these things sooner, I could have saved myself a lot of heartache.

On March 19, 2006, I was ordained in my church by the Franklin Conference of Free Will Baptists. It was an exciting day in my life but bittersweet at the same time. I remember thinking how much I wished Kristy could have been there. She was always such a support to me, and I missed her so much. I prayed and asked God to please let her know that mom and dad were still working for Him and we looked forward to seeing her and Dani again some sweet day.

Shortly after my ordination I once again began doubting my abilities to minister. I had a friend, Pastor Gary Whaley who had lost a son, David, six years earlier. David was twenty-nine years old when he died from a surgical error. He laid in the hospital for fourteen days before he passed away. I don't know why I didn't go talk with Pastor Gary sooner but the Lord now impressed it upon me to go see him. I knew that Gary would know exactly how I felt and I thought maybe he could shed some light on some things for me or at least help me put things in their proper perspective concerning the ministry.

I met with Gary a few times, and he and his wife, Shirley, went to dinner with Steph and me one evening. We had a great time of fellowship and it felt good to just talk with another couple who knew the pain and suffering we had experienced. I am forever grateful to Gary and Shirley for ministering to us as they did.

I met with Gary about a week or so later in his office, and he told me about his struggle of continuing on after David's untimely death. Talking with Gary helped me realize that every emotion or feeling I experienced was absolutely normal. During his own time of suffering Gary told me how the Lord spoke a verse of Scripture to his heart that helped him immensely. It is found in Psalm 46:10: *"Be still and know that I am God."* I have since claimed the truth of that verse for my own comfort and healing. God is aware of what is happening in our lives, and He has not forgotten us. He wants us to just trust in Him. When we learn to do that, miracles start happening.

Before leaving Gary's office that morning he told me a few other things that really helped me. I had told him earlier that I was trying hard to get through this ordeal, but I felt like I was failing with every move I made. He told me that I needed to quit trying and to let the Lord take over. I didn't really grasp hold of the importance of that statement at first, but when it finally sank in, it made a huge difference in the way I started approaching everything that I did. I had been putting pressure on myself in trying not to let Steph down, the people in my church, and even God Himself. Instead of trusting in God to work through me, I was trying to do everything on my own. I was getting burned out, because I was not waiting on God in the things I was trying to accomplish.

The second thing Gary told me has never stopped speaking to my heart. He said that if I would allow God, He would build my ministry upon Kristy's death. Admittedly, he said that may be hard to digest at first, and he encouraged me to allow God to take that statement and speak to my heart. There is not a day that goes by that I don't think about those words my good friend gave to me. If we will allow Him, God will take our greatest trials and use them to build us into strong vessels for His use. What Gary told me makes so much sense. I know that, because of what we have been through, Steph and I can be of help to others who may be going through the same kind of hurt. We both want God to use us in any way He so desires. It will be uplifting to the name of Jesus Christ, and it will also allow Kristy and Dani's deaths to not be in vain.

I noticed a change in my prayer life. I was now starting to listen to God more so than before. For too long I was telling Him what I wanted or what I needed. The Holy Spirit was now impressing upon my spirit to listen to what God wanted to speak to me.

Prayer is more than just talking to God. Prayer is more than just bringing requests and petitions to His attention. Prayer should also include listening. God is not a robot that is programmed to meet our selfish whims and demands. We also need to hear what He is saying to us. Could you imagine a relationship where only one person does all the talking and the other one never says anything? It's no different with God. Being His child gives us a unique relationship with our Creator. He certainly desires to hear our requests of Him, but He also wants to speak to us as well.

God started speaking to me about Steph. One of the things He showed me was how I needed to spend more time with her. I had always felt like we had a good strong marriage, but losing Kristy had taken its toll on us. Without even realizing it we had slowly drifted apart, and the Lord was telling me that we needed to restore our relationship with one another.

I went to Pastor Tim and told him that I needed to take a break from ministry for a while and to work on getting mine and Steph's relationship back to where it needed to be. Unless a marriage is in harmony, both naturally and spiritually, a person's ministry can never be truly successful.

Over the next couple of months I continued to seek the Lord for direction and told Him that I only wanted to fulfill His will for mine and Steph's lives. I believe we have made great strides in our relationship. We sit and talk with one another like we used to. We try to put Christ at the center of all that we do. We know that our lives will never be the same again, but we also have the assurance that God will see us through to the end.

One night while in prayer, the Lord spoke something to my heart. It couldn't have been any clearer if He had spoken it audibly. I was telling Him how much I longed for heaven. I continued praying and telling the Lord that I missed Kristy so much and longed for the day when I would see her again. I mentioned this to God often during my prayer times. In fact, that had become one of my favorite things to tell Him.

As I was praying that night God stopped me in what seemed like mid-sentence. He then spoke this to my heart: "When you long to see me more than you do Kristy, then my son, you will discover the real joy of serving me." It hit me like the ton of proverbial bricks that we so often speak about. There was nothing wrong with longing to see my daughter again, but I had put my desires of wanting to see her ahead of longing to be with God. In His loving way, the Lord let me know that I can put nothing ahead of Him and still be pleasing to Him, and that also included Kristy.

That was a real spiritual eye-opener for me. You see, as much as I love Kristy and desire to see her again, I must always keep in mind that it wasn't her who died for me. Jesus Christ is the One who gave His life for me so that I may live in heaven throughout eternity. Without Jesus doing what He did, neither Kristy nor I would have had the opportunity to spend eternity in heaven and this conversation would be moot. Since that night when God brought that truth to my attention, my prayer life has changed as well as the way I live my life. God has to be first in everything that we do. When we fail to put Him first, you can be assured that spiritual disaster is soon to follow.

The titles of the last two chapters was, "Where Are You Lord?" The answer to that question is, "Right here beside you my child." God promised us in His Word that He would never allow us to go through the storms of this life alone. I have found His promise to be true.

Chapter 9

The Magnitude of God's Grace

He stood, and measured the earth: he beheld, and drove asunder the nations; and the everlasting mountains were scattered, the perpetual hills did bow: his ways are everlasting.
(Habakkuk 3:6)

I am going to attempt to talk about the grace of God. I say attempt because God's grace is just too complex to understand in its entirety. The irony of this complex word, though, is that when we trust in God, grace reveals itself in a way that is simple to comprehend. For example, *"For by grace are ye saved through faith; and that not of yourselves: it is the gift of God"* (Ephesians 2:8). Salvation comes only through and by the grace of God. This grace is simply accepting what Jesus Christ has already done for you and me. If salvation could be obtained through or by anything you or I could do, then salvation by grace would cease to be possible. In short, grace is God doing for us what we are unable to do for ourselves. It gets even more extraordinary when you study about grace.

The word grace is found one-hundred and sixty-six times in the Bible. It is first mentioned in Genesis 6:8, *"But*

Noah found grace in the eyes of the Lord." I'm sure you know the story. God was about to destroy all of mankind and every other living creature upon the face of the earth. He looked down in His grace and mercy and saved one man and His family. While looking upon Noah, God also saw the generations to follow down through the remainder of the ages, including you and me. Did God save Noah because He deserved it? No, it was because of His grace. As a matter of fact, when you look up the word grace, it comes from the Hebrew word *chanan*, and it means "*to find favor, to stoop in kindness to an inferior.*" Just as Jesus Christ, the Son of God, lowered Himself to be born in human form, God the Father lowered Himself to save those who were undeserving of His matchless love and grace. That's the kind of God we serve.

Though I feel inadequate to teach or write about the vastness of God's remarkable grace, I do want to share with you what my Heavenly Father has shown me concerning this part of His personality. I pray that what He has shown me will be of benefit to you in some way.

Grace and mercy are just two of the many attributes of our Heavenly Father. Each one of His attributes spells out love because that is exactly what God is. Each one of us is a recipient of God's grace and mercy. The best descriptions I have ever heard for these two words are as follows: *Grace* is God giving us what we don't deserve, and *mercy* is God withholding from us what we do deserve. As simple as those descriptions are it's still not possible to understand the entire personality of God in our present mortal make-up. I wrote something in the introduction of this book that I believe is worth repeating:

Why can't we fully understand all there is to know about God in this life? It is because His love, mercy, and grace are too far-reaching and so much more than the human, finite mind can even begin to comprehend or understand.

God's grace covers every circumstance, obstacle, problem, or sin with which man ever came into contact. His grace covers what each individual, all of whom He created, may need during his or her span of life on this earth. I'm talking about grace that will see us through all of life's trials, temptations, struggles and battles.

We must realize that each person needs God's grace extended to them in a way that is unique, in a way that only He can do. For this reason it's impossible to understand the part of God's grace that supplies or sustains an individual at his or her needed time or moment. In turn, it's impossible for you to understand the grace which carries me through my most needed moment and vice versa.

God made each one of us differently, and each one is unique in our Heavenly Father's eyes. Therefore, each person will face different tests and trials during their lifetime on this earth. Every test, trial, temptation, or obstacle that we face requires our Heavenly Father's grace to sustain us, and each time that we come through those difficult times, we will gain a better understanding of our omniscient, omnipotent, and omnipresent, yet, reachable God. Unless a person were exposed to every test, trial, temptation, obstacle, problem, or sin that was ever known to man, it would be impossible for them to know God in His entirety.

Right now we see through a glass darkly. We only see and comprehend what we personally need for us as individuals, which means that we have to live by faith. Thank God, though, one glorious day, we will see and understand Him in His fullness. Until then, we must learn to love and appreciate what we do know and understand and to not question what we don't know and don't understand. Only then will we be able to experience the peace, joy, and contentment of serving God, which He intends for us to know in this life.

Both you and I have experienced many different aspects of God's grace. I know about His saving grace. I know about grace that has let me endure sickness, loss of employment, and lack of income which has created a financial burden. Each time I faced one of those storms, I came away with a better knowledge and understanding of my Heavenly Father.

There are things in life which I have never experienced though, and consequently, I don't have an understanding of the kind of grace required to endure those particular storms. For instance, I don't know about the grace required to get through a divorce, the loss of a spouse, or a parent. I think about people who have lost houses, loved ones, and every personal item they ever owned due to tornados, hurricanes, earthquakes, etc. I have never needed the kind of grace required to get through something of that nature.

When God took Kristy and Dani, I came to a knowledge of grace I never knew before. It really is hard to explain what takes place within one's self when grace is given that you have never previously experienced. When God saturates you with that particular kind of grace, there is something supernatural which takes over your spirit and being. You realize that something is carrying you through a time when you are unable to help yourself. There is an inner peace which passes all understanding (Philippians 4:7). This kind of grace brings comfort to the troubled heart when you felt that there was no way to be comforted. Even during times of sadness and heartbreak, there is still a joy in the Lord which is unexplainable and undeniable. Even as I write this I'm struggling to find the words to make sense of what I am trying to say about God's unfathomable grace. The best I can say is that when God distributes this kind of grace upon the one in need of it, it can only be understood by that individual or by someone else who has experienced it as well.

As I have learned about God's grace and accepted the healing power that comes with it, I have become more aware of the vastness of His grace. Some people have expressed to me that they didn't know how Steph and I ever got through the loss of our daughter and granddaughter. As much as we have suffered through this terrible tragedy, there really is great consolation in knowing they are in heaven. We are going to see them again, and what a joy that is to think upon.

I have often said that had Kristy not been saved I don't think I could have gotten through that storm. To think that my child would be lost forever is almost unbearable to me. That is something I have never experienced. I don't know what it's like to lose a child who is unsaved. That kind of loss requires an even different kind of grace than what Steph and I needed to get through Kristy and Dani's deaths. God also has that kind of grace, and it is freely given to those parents who are in need of it. The bottom line of what I am trying to say is this: God has grace to cover every circumstance that we may ever experience.

Grace is a beautiful word. Since the beginning of creation man has been in need of God's grace just to survive. God's grace spans all heaven and earth in its ability to answer all of man's problems. Grace runs the spiritual gamut, so to speak: salvation, deliverance, protection, healing, and whatever else may try to separate us from God and His remarkable love.

The purpose of grace is to keep man in a position with God in which he may attain eternal salvation. Without grace none of us would even have the slightest hope of being saved. Over the next few chapters I want us to look closely at three aspects of God's grace. Let's start with the magnitude of God's grace.

The magnitude of God and His grace goes far beyond the range of our mental comprehension. When I think of God's grace, I am reminded of the human body. God made us with a built-in immune system that is truly amazing to say the least. For instance, let's consider the blood in our human bodies and the immune system that it provides for us. Blood contains four major parts:

- Red blood cells - carry oxygen from your lungs to your body cells and carbon dioxide from your body cells back to your lungs to be exhaled
- Platelets - help clot blood
- White blood cells - fight germs that infect the body
- Plasma - the fluid portion of the blood which transports all of the other blood cells throughout the body

Your immune system is like an army that protects you from disease.

- Your skin is the first wall of protection against foreign invaders that cause disease
- The second line of defense are fluids like mucus found in your respiratory system and tears from your eyes
- If the invaders do pass through these defenses then there is an army battalion of white blood cells and their weapons that fight against germs
- Helper Tcells - act as the "lookout" for your body by recognizing invaders and then sending signals to the other white blood cells
- Bcells - make antibodies to smother the invaders once they receive the signals from the helper Tcells

- Killer Tcells - kill the invaders once they receive the signals from the helper Tcells
- Phagocytes - act as "eating" cells. They destroy invaders with chemicals and then eat them

Just as the blood immune system in our human bodies fights off sickness and disease, God's grace fights off the onslaughts of the enemy in his desire to destroy us. The only difference is that sometimes our immune systems fail us, and we still get sickness and disease. God's grace is always victorious against anything and everything that comes against us.

Let's look at a few examples in the Bible of what I am talking about:

In Genesis 1:26 we learn of God's creation of man. From the creation of Adam to Adam's help meet (Eve, his wife), whom God made from the rib of Adam's side in Genesis 2:21, it's instantly brought to our attention God's desire to meet the needs of His most prized possession on earth. In Genesis 2:8, God planted a garden in Eden, and the Scriptures tell us that is where He put the man whom He had formed.

The Garden of Eden, we are told, was a place where Adam and Eve could have all they needed for life and happiness, all that was good and pleasant, and God allowed them to enjoy it in abundance.

God placed only one restriction on Adam and Eve. They were not to eat of the tree of the knowledge of good and evil, which was in the garden. He warned them that if they did eat of that tree they would die. Eating of this forbidden tree would result in their natural deaths years later, but the greater emphasis was placed upon the spiritual death they would encounter because of their disobedience. Their lack of obedience to God's command resulted in their being removed from the garden (the place where they lacked for nothing) and being put in the world as we now know it (a world of sin and separation from God).

Adam and Eve were no longer in continual communion with their Creator, and sad to say, that wasn't the end of it. Their sin of disobedience was now passed on to their children and every other person born into the human race, including you and me. Because of Adam and Eve's sin, all of us fall under the curse that was placed upon them. We are all born with that same sin nature, because we are no longer a part of Adam, the sinless man. We are a part of the sinful and disobedient Adam who fell in the garden. When we are born, my friend, we are born into a sinful and corrupt world that is at odds against the Creator of this universe.

Paul explains this best in his letter to the Roman church. In Romans 3:23, the apostle writes, *"For all have sinned, and come short of the glory of God."* Many people stumble at this and don't want to admit any wrongdoing on their part, but the Holy Bible teaches otherwise. Again, plain and simple, because of our first natural father's (Adam) sin, we all inherit his sin nature and are without hope of going to heaven unless someone pays the penalty to set us free from our bondage. Thank God someone did!

The bottom line to this sad story is that Adam and Eve are now lost and without hope of ever communing with God again. If you don't know this story then I hope you will read the book of Genesis. It will not only enlighten you as to how we got here today, but it shows us our hope for tomorrow and throughout eternity.

Now let's see God's grace at work. God wasn't pleased that Adam and Eve now had to be removed from the garden. You may ask, "Then why didn't He just overlook their one little mistake and give them a second chance?" Because God is perfect and sinless. He cannot have a relationship with anyone that is associated with sin that has not been redeemed by Him. By this I mean there is a penalty that must be paid because of sin, and until that penalty is paid for, no one can have a personal relationship with their Creator.

God loved His creation so much (that includes you and me) that He immediately made an escape for Adam and Eve's wrongdoing. In today's language God created a spiritual loophole so that Adam and his new wife could have a second chance. This loophole is for our second chance as well. Without it we would be destined for eternal punishment because of our sins. In chapter three of Genesis, God explains that He is going to devise a plan that will thwart Satan's attempt to destroy mankind forever by sending someone to defeat him once and for all.

Genesis 3:15 says, *"And I will put enmity between thee and the woman, and between thy seed and her seed: it shall bruise thy head, and thou shalt bruise his heel."* This passage of Scripture is God's first promise of redemption to fallen man. What God is promising is the future coming of Jesus Christ into a sinful world. Christ will be born in human form, become a man, present Himself as the Messiah, and will ultimately be crucified, thus paying the penalty of sin for all of creation. His vicarious death will enable man to once again be reunited with God the Father. What a wonderful picture of grace in action!

Space doesn't permit me to write all the examples the Bible gives us of God's remarkable grace. I will share a few of the more prominent ones, though, and I encourage you to go read and study for yourself the love our Heavenly Father has for His creation. Remember, our Creator loves you as much as He does those whom He showered His grace upon in the Bible. Also, remember that, *"God is not a respecter of persons"* (Acts 10:34). In other words, He won't do for one what He won't do for another.

God's Word is full of stories of men and women who made mistake after mistake and were given a second chance.

We serve a God who is not tolerant of sin but at the same time He gives ample opportunity for repentance to all who seek His forgiveness.

Let's take a closer look at God's extraordinary grace at work in ordinary people.

Noah - In Genesis 9:21, we are told that Noah planted a vineyard and yielded to the temptation of drunkenness. Noah had a weakness in his flesh, but he was still a saved man by God's grace. Here was a man whom God used to start the human race completely over again after the flood. In spite of the weaknesses in this great man of God, his faith saved him by God's grace.

Jacob - A study of Jacob reveals that he cheated his brother out of his birthright (Genesis 25:29-34) and even deceived his own aged father (Genesis 27:1-29). Jacob could have been easily identified as untrustworthy, a liar, a swindler, and a crook. Yet, God brought this man to a place of repentance, and he became recognized as one of the patriarchs of the Bible. The Jewish people refer to God as the God of their fathers Abraham, Isaac, and their father Jacob. God changed Jacob's name to "Israel" which among one of its meanings is "Prince with God."

Joseph - Though Joseph's father loved Joseph more than he loved Joseph's brethren and Joseph was one who desired to please God, his inability to demonstrate humility toward his brothers for all that God showed him proved to be his downfall (Genesis, chapter 37). Joseph didn't fall into sin and temptation to the same degree as many others that we read about, but his story is still one which displays the remarkable grace of God at work in one of His servants who had to learn the hard way. God used Joseph to save the whole nation of Israel.

David - David went down in history as the greatest of all of Israel's kings. Here was a man who even God Himself said was a *"man after God's own heart"* (1 Samuel 13:14). Yet, this great man and king committed adultery and murder, two of the most despicable sins known to mankind (2 Samuel, chapters 11 and 12). Yet, God forgave David after he repented. David exhibited what true remorse and repentance really are. Read Psalm 51, and you will get a first-hand view of a sorrowful heart coming back to God and his God forgiving Him. God's grace knows no limitations.

Moses - Moses killed a man (Exodus 2:11,12), argued with God over His decision to call him for service (Exodus 3:11-4:13), and sinned against God through disobedience (Numbers 20:7-13); yet, God used this great prophet to lead the whole nation of Israel out of Egyptian bondage while preparing them to enter the Promised Land.

Jonah - In Jonah we find grace exhibited in a way that many of us have a hard time understanding. Jonah was a prophet who God told to go to Nineveh, the Assyrian capital, and warn them of coming destruction if they didn't repent. The Assyrians were enemies of the Jewish people. Jonah didn't want them to be warned, so he got on a ship and went in the opposite direction. God caused a fierce storm to erupt, forcing the crew on board to toss cargo from the ship, including Jonah. A great fish swallowed Jonah, where he remained for three days. God ordered the fish to vomit Jonah up onto dry ground, and from there he walked to Nineveh to deliver God's message. You may be wondering where God's grace is in Jonah's story. Understand that God could have just judged Jonah for his disobedience and let him die on the open sea. Rather, though, He saved Jonah to complete His will for his life. This was a tough lesson for Jonah to learn, but grace can sometimes seem hard when we are running from God. The ultimate work of grace is to save us from hurt or destruction. God's grace is often unexplainable in its operation.

Peter - Here was a man who possibly made more mistakes than any of the disciples who followed after Jesus. Not only did Peter often speak out of turn, but several times he was openly rebuked by the Lord. He showed a lack of faith when Christ invited him to walk out to Him on the open sea, and more times than one could imagine he was overzealous when he should have been silent while learning from Jesus. On the night of Christ's crucifixion, three times Peter even denied knowing His Savior (John 18:18-27), just as Jesus told him he would do (John 13:38). It is a beautiful picture of Christ forgiving Peter in John 21:15-18 and giving him instructions for future ministry. Peter went on to become one of the greatest leaders in the church's history, all because of God's grace.

Paul - Once a fiery Pharisee with only one mission in mind, Paul set out to kill as many followers of Jesus Christ as he possibly could. One day while traveling on the Damascus Road, Paul was hit by a light so intense that it blinded him. That light was Jesus Christ, and He told Paul that He had a work for Him to do (Acts, chapter 22). Paul went on to become the greatest of all the apostles, writing more than half of the books in the New Testament. This great man of God started numerous churches for Christ while being persecuted, beaten, shipwrecked, and ultimately martyred by being beheaded. Only God's grace can cause a person to be willing to give his own life for Jesus Christ after they had once had people killed for the same reason. This kind of grace considers dying for the Lord an honor. Being warned of future persecution Paul replied, "*I am ready not to be bound only, but also to die at Jerusalem for the name of the*

Lord Jesus" (Acts 21:13). There is no sin that grace cannot forgive.

John Mark - By many people's standards John Mark had been considered a failure in his early years as a Christian. John Mark accompanied Paul and Barnabus on their first missionary journey. For some unknown reason John Mark left and went back home much to the displeasure of Paul. In fact, Paul refused to take John Mark along again when they were ready to start their second journey. Paul considered John Mark a failure in his attempt to be a missionary. No doubt, John Mark received much criticism for his departure on the first trip. Barnabus still believed in him, though, and gave him the second chance that he deserved. Certainly, God forgave John Mark, and because of grace he went on to be a huge asset to the spreading of the gospel for Jesus Christ. Even Paul later admitted that John Mark was a profitable servant in the ministry (2 Timothy 4:11). He would eventually write the second of the gospels in the New Testament. When others are ready to throw the towel in on you, grace will make you useful for Christ.

Truly, grace knows no boundaries or limitations in providing hope, comfort, or salvation to a lost and hurting soul. Grace is never late in its ability to give the necessary touch at just the right time. Though we often reject God's grace in His attempt to save, sustain, heal, touch, rescue, or provide comfort to a hurting heart, it doesn't mean that grace wasn't there for us. Too often we just simply refuse His grace.

Chapter 10

The Mystery of God's Grace

Verily thou art a God that hidest thyself, O God of Israel, the Savior.
(Isaiah 45:15)

Grace would not be such a mystery if its recipients were worthy of receiving it. Quite honestly, though, that is one of the mysteries of grace. God pours out this unique part of Himself upon a people who are undeserving of it.

That is exactly what makes grace so hard to accept by many people. Human nature often prevents us from forgiving those who have wronged us. Because of this we sometimes find it hard to believe that God would really forgive or heal us. Forgiveness in itself is not an attribute that the natural man possesses. True forgiveness is found only in a heart for God.

God Himself is a mystery to mankind. It is a mystery how an infinite God would lower Himself to become like His own finite creation. It is a mystery how the Lord Jesus Christ died upon a cross for sins that He never committed. It's a mystery how he was willing to forgive even the very ones who were responsible for His death on that cross. It's another mystery how the Lord Jesus is also willing to forgive us as well. Though we may have not been there physically driving the nails or shouting, "Crucify Him! Crucify Him," we are still guilty by association through our first father, Adam.

The mysteries of God make up the entire New Testament. The Holy Bible speaks of at least eleven mysteries of God in the New Testament. A few of them are as follows: the mystery of the kingdom of heaven (Matthew 13:3-50), the mystery of the New Testament church as one body composed of Jews and Gentiles (Ephesians 3:1-12; Romans 16:25; Ephesians 6:19; Colossians 4:3), the mystery of the church as the bride of Christ (Ephesians 5:23-32), the mystery of Christ as the incarnate fullness of the Godhead embodied, in whom all the divine wisdom for man subsists (1 Corinthians 2:7; Colossians 2:2,9).

All of these make up the mystery of God in whom we have limited understanding. Quite possibly, the greatest mystery of all is the working of God's grace. Do you remember our earlier definition of grace? Grace is God giving us what we do not deserve. Let's take a closer look through Scripture at some examples of undeserved grace that has been offered to us if we are only willing to accept it:

> For *by grace are ye saved* through faith; and that not of yourselves: it is the gift of God: Not of works, lest any man should boast. (Ephesians 2:8,9)

It's important to realize that there is absolutely nothing we in ourselves can do to attain salvation. You cannot give enough money to the church to be saved. You cannot help the poor enough to be saved. You cannot attend church enough to be saved. You cannot do enough good works to earn heaven as your eternal dwelling place. Salvation comes only through and by the grace of God.

Notice Ephesians 2:9, again. If there was something we could do to deserve salvation, we would then be able to boast that it was us who earned our salvation and not Christ who saved us. By grace alone, through faith, are we saved.

> *I am crucified with Christ: nevertheless I live; yet not I but Christ liveth in me: and the life which I now live in the flesh I live by the faith of the son of God, who loved me, and gave himself for me.* (Galatians 2:20)

Because of grace, we now have access to saving faith. The faith of the Son of God "*loved me*" and "*gave Himself*" for me. I like the way J. Vernon McGee explained this:

> Christ loved me, but He could not love me into heaven. He had to give Himself for me. The gift of God is eternal life in Christ Jesus. You can only receive a gift by faith. This applies to any gift, for that matter. You have to believe that the giver who holds out the gift to you is sincere. You must believe that he is telling the truth when he holds it out to you and says, "It is yours." You have to reach out in faith and take it before it belongs to you. God offers you the gift of eternal life in Christ Jesus.

> *Even the mystery which hath been hid from ages and from generations, but now is made manifest to his saints: To whom God would make known what is the riches of the glory of this mystery among the Gentiles; which is Christ in you, the hope of glory* (Colossians 1:26,27)

The mystery which Paul is speaking about, here, is the fact that salvation is available to everyone who will receive it. "*Christ in you, the hope of glory*"—we are in Christ Jesus.

The moment you put your trust in the Lord Jesus Christ, you are saved and in the family of God. This amazing truth is still a mystery to many people.

> *And without controversy <u>great is the mystery of godliness</u>: God was manifest in the flesh, justified in the Spirit, seen of angels, preached unto the Gentiles, believed on in the world, received up into glory.* (1 Timothy 3:16)

The mystery of godliness is that the person of Jesus Christ entered this world in which we live, paid the penalty of sin, and now makes men and women alike godly as He is. We live in a world which teaches that nothing is free. This belief also exists where God is concerned. The mystery of salvation confuses multitudes of people into believing that being saved must somehow depend upon their own works or by simply just being a good person. The mystery is solved when one understands that the price of salvation has already been paid for in the work of Jesus Christ by His death upon the cross.

In order to get even an inkling of understanding grace, we need to better understand the attributes of our Heavenly Father. Consider these facts concerning the person of God:

- God is self-existent. Exodus 3:13,14
- God is self-sufficient. Psalms 50:10-12
- God is eternal. Deuteronomy 33:27; Psalms 90:2
- God is infinite. 1 Kings 8:22-27; Jeremiah 23:24
- God is omnipresent. Psalms 139:7-12
- God is omnipotent. Genesis 18:14; Revelation 19:16
- God is omniscient. Psalms 139:2-6; Isaiah 40:13,14
- God is wise. Proverbs 3:19; 1 Timothy 1:17
- God is immutable. Hebrews 1:10-12; 13:8

- God is sovereign. Isaiah 46:9-11
- God is incomprehensible. Job 11:7-19; Romans 11:33
- God is holy. Leviticus 19:2; 1 Peter 1:15
- God is righteous and just. Psalms 119:137
- God is true. John 17:3; Titus 1:1,2
- God is faithful. Deuteronomy 7:9; Psalms 89:1,2
- God is light. James 1:17; 1 John 1:5
- God is good. Psalms 107:8
- God is merciful. Psalms 103:8-17
- God is gracious. Psalms 111:4; 1 Peter 5:10
- God is love. John 3:16; Romans 5:8
- God is spirit. John 4:24
- God is one. Deuteronomy 6:4:5; Isaiah 44:6-8
- God is a Trinity. Matthew 28:19; 2 Corinthians 13:14

Our Creator is sovereign in every aspect. There is absolutely nothing that escapes His knowledge. Consider the following list of things which God sees and knows:

- He sees all things. Proverbs 15:3
- He knows the size and scope of the universe. Psalm 147:4
- He knows about the animal creation. Mathew 10:29
- He knows mankind. Matthew 10:30
- He knows our thoughts. Psalms 139:2; 44:21
- He knows our words. Psalms 139:4
- He knows our deeds. Psalms 139:2
- He knows our sorrows. Exodus 3:7
- He knows our needs. Matthew 6:32
- He knows our devotions. Genesis 18:17-19; 22:11,12, 2 Chronicles 16:9
- He knows out frailties. Psalms 103:14
- He knows our foolishness. Psalms 69:5

- He knows His own. John 10:14; 2 Timothy 2:19
- He knows the past, present, and future. Acts 15:18
- He knows what might or could have been. Matthew 11:23

Our God is everything that we need. His many names testify of His greatness and sufficiency for His creation. He is:

1. "Elohim" meaning "God," a reference to God's power and might. Genesis 1:1; 19:1
2. "Adonai" meaning "Lord," a reference to the Lordship of God. Malachi 1:6
3. "Jehovah" a reference to God's divine salvation. Genesis 2:4
4. "Jehovah-Maccaddeshem" meaning "The Lord thy sanctifier." Exodus 31:13
5. "Jehovah-Rohi" meaning "The Lord my shepherd." Psalms 23:1
6. "Jehovah-Shammah" meaning "The Lord who is present." Ezekiel 48:35
7. "Jehovah-Rapha" meaning "The Lord our healer." Exodus 16:26
8. "Jehovah-Tsidkenu" meaning "The Lord our righteousness." Jeremiah 23:6
9. "Jehovah-Jireh" meaning "The Lord will provide." Genesis 22:13,14
10. "Jehovah-Nissi" meaning "The Lord our banner." Exodus 17:5
11. "Jehovah-Shalom" meaning "The Lord is peace." Judges 6:24
12. "Jehovah-Sabbaoth" meaning "The Lord of Hosts." Isaiah 6:1-3
13. "El-Elyon" meaning "The most high God." Genesis 14:17-20; Isaiah 14:13,14

14. "El-Roi" meaning "The strong one who sees." Genesis 16:12
15. "El-Shaddai" meaning "The God of the mountains" or "God Almighty." Genesis 17:1; Psalms 91:1
16. "El-Olam" meaning "The Everlasting God." Isaiah 40:28-31

I hope these lists, which tell of our Heavenly Father's personality, traits, and attributes, help give you a better understanding of His remarkable character. There is none like unto Him. He is God and God alone. Even yet, to have this knowledge of His divine being still leaves us far short of comprehending His amazing grace. Much of God is still a mystery to our finite minds.

For example, let's consider the mystery of the forgiveness of sins. Yes, I know that if you are a born-again Christian, you realize that He has forgiven you and your sins are now covered by the blood of Jesus. The forgiveness of our sins is only the beginning of the work of grace. Now look at what God says about our sinful past:

"I, even I, am he that blotteth out thy transgressions for mine own sake, and will not remember thy sins." (Isaiah 43:25)

"As far as the east is from the west, so far hath he removed our transgressions from us." (Psalms 103:12)

Think for a moment about what these verses of Scripture are saying. Not only does God forgive our sins but He forgets them as well. What God is saying here is that once forgiven, He will never again bring up our sinful past. This is a trick the devil tries to pull on us. He is good to remind us of things

137

we have done in the past so that we will feel shameful, or unworthy of God's love, but God just turns to us and says, "I don't know what you are talking about. You are forgiven my child, and your sins are no longer remembered."

This is grace that most of us struggle with. You see, grace chooses not only to forgive; grace also forgets. How many times do we say that we have forgiven someone, only to continually bring up what they did to us in the past? If we truly forgive someone then we won't dwell on the past.

Another mystery of the grace of forgiveness is that God's grace has no limitations. A great illustration of this is found in Matthew, chapter 18.

In this story Peter comes to Jesus and asks how many times would be appropriate for him to forgive his brother who has sinned against him. Then Peter, thinking that surely the Lord would be proud of him, says to Jesus, "*till seven times?*"

Jesus then blows Peter and the others away with His answer to this question. Jesus responds by saying to him, "*I say not unto thee, Until seven times: but, Until seventy times seven.*"

Most of us have a breaking point when it comes to how many times we are going to forgive someone who has wronged us. God and His grace forgives as long as we are sincere toward Him in our repentance. We are to do likewise with our brothers and sisters.

When we do sin, grace covers those mortal weaknesses and shortcomings as well. 1 John 1:9 says, "*If we confess our sins, he is faithful and just to forgive us our sins, and to cleanse us from all unrighteousness.*"

Again I say, there are no boundaries or limitations to the power of God's grace.

I hope you are beginning to see the magnitude of God's grace. I have experienced many aspects of God's grace. Aside from His saving grace, I would have to say that God's healing grace was the most powerful internal force I have ever encountered.

That Sunday evening when we were in Pastor Tim's office and learned that Dani had died in the accident, I literally fell apart. I got up out of my chair, my knees buckled, and I just went to the floor. As I lay there in a prostrate position, I cried out to God, "Oh God. You promised that you would put nothing on us that we would not be able to bear. I can't bear this Lord." I never heard an audible voice, but it couldn't have been any clearer what the Holy Spirit spoke to my heart. He whispered to me, "I know you can't my child, but I can."

Did the pain go away? No. Did I stop hurting? No. Did I suddenly have an understanding of why this happened? No. I did experience a peace that I could not explain, though. As bad as I hurt at that very moment, I knew that God was with me and that somehow I was going to make it through this. I am here today to tell you that He kept His promise to me. If you are reading this and need a touch from God, today, I want you to know that He will see you through. That is His promise, and God never has, nor ever will, break His promises to us: *"there hath not failed one word of all his good promise"* (1 Kings 8:56).

Chapter 11

The Misconception of God's Grace

The Lord is righteous in all his ways, and holy in all his works.
(Psalm 145:17)

All of the mysteries of God and grace leads us to the topic of the many misconceptions of His grace. The false ideas and wrong opinions shared by all of us about our sometimes incomprehensible God are often many, to say the least. I'm only going to touch on three misconceptions that sometimes plague Christians. Notice that I said Christians. I'm talking about misconceptions by believers, not unbelievers. The misconceptions by unbelievers are understandable. One cannot expect someone who has no personal relationship with God to understand His ways and workings. The believer, on the other hand, is often hung up by his or her own ideas of how they think things should be and not necessarily how Scripture teaches. This can lead to serious problems in our Christian walk.

The three misconceptions of grace I want to address are as follows:

- Bad things don't happen to Christians
- God's grace is automatic for the believer
- Grace eliminates the pain and hurt of the believer

Bad things don't happen to Christians.

We often say that we know that just because we are a Christian, we are not assured that bad things won't happen to us. In reality, though, when tragedy strikes, or something happens which turns our world upside-down, we're prone to go to God in bewilderment as if to say, "Lord, I don't understand how you could allow this to be happening to me."

It's much easier to look at someone else's situation without questioning God, or at least we are a lot quicker to make such statements as, "*God will see you through this*," or "*Keep the faith, friend*," or "*God's grace is sufficient*."

Can I share a little secret with you? When you are going through the worst time of your life, there are few words, if any, that will bring encouragement to your troubled heart. Once again, in dealing with Kristy and Dani's deaths, the only two comments that even remotely made sense to me were, "I'm praying for you" and "I just don't know what to say." Everything else was just empty words. During those moments I was comforted by countless friends and family, but my most desperate need was a touch that only God could give. I needed grace that only He could provide.

In my mind I always feared the thought of anything ever happening to Kristy, Matt, or one of my grandchildren. Truthfully though, I guess I thought being a Christian gave me an advantage that unbelievers do not have. I thought that because I was a child of God He would not allow anything so terrible as a tragic death to happen to a family member so close to me. It didn't matter that I knew that Christians are killed everyday and family members are left behind to endure the pain and suffering that I now know.

You see, though, that was different. I knew that God's grace would see *them* through. All *they* had to do was keep the faith. God would see *them* through because His grace is sufficient. Boy, have *I* learned a whole lot over these past few years.

Please remember and hold tightly onto this next statement. If tragedy strikes you, get prepared for the greatest spiritual battle of your life. Satan will be standing close by whispering in your ear, "What kind of God would allow something like this to happen? Do you still really believe that He cares about you?" Believe me when I say that Satan's vicious onslaughts never cease. At that particular moment it's easy to become weak in your faith and vulnerable to his deceit and lies. Only God can rescue you from the snares of the enemy.

Yes, my friend bad things can and do happen to Christians, just as they do to unbelievers. We are not assured that life will always bring smiles and laughter. As a matter of fact, the book of Job teaches us that *"Man that is born of a woman is of few days, and full of trouble"* (Job 14:1). God has not lied to us. We have often just been guilty of not opening ourselves up to receiving the whole truth.

I don't want to paint a picture of gloom, here. I hope you are not reading this and saying, "Then what is the use of being a Christian? They are just as prone to bad things happening to them as non-Christians."

Being a Christian has every advantage over the unbeliever. The benefits are too numerous to write about and would require many more books and authors to describe them all. Though Christians are not protected from everything bad that life has to throw at us, we are sheltered by God's grace to endure anything that comes our way.

I have heard Christians witness to unbelievers and lead them to believe that, if they give their heart to the Lord, all of their troubles will go away. That is simply not true. I tell people that when you get saved you now have a way of coping with everything that troubled you before. Trusting in God will provide you the grace to overcome those things which plagued you before. God is not a great magician; He is the great physician.

I feel inadequate to put into words what I want to say about the enduring power of God's grace. It cannot be explained, it must be experienced to understand it. I know that I would not have survived my tragedy without His healing grace. It's unexplainable, but let me try as best as I can. Do I still hurt? Yes. Do I still miss Kristy and Dani terribly? Yes. Are some days still worse than others? Yes. Do I feel closer to God now than I ever did? Yes. Has my faith grown? Yes. Is there a peace in my heart that I cannot explain? Yes. You explain it to me if you can.

God's grace is automatic for the believer.

The second misconception involves the distribution of God's grace upon His people. The false teaching of prosperity is rampant among many Christians and churches today. This false doctrine teaches that God will bless you with financial wealth if you give to their ministries. People are often hoodwinked into believing that God has to meet their whims and demands because that is what His Word teaches. These same teachers would also lead you to believe that God's grace is freely poured out upon everyone, regardless of their spiritual condition or attitude toward God. God doesn't force His grace upon anyone. Let me explain what I mean by this.

If you are a born-again Christian, you understand that was a choice you made. God never made you accept Him as your personal Savior. John 3:16 is probably the most quoted verse in all the Bible: "*For God so loved the world, that he gave his only begotten Son, that <u>whosoever</u> believeth in him should not perish, but have everlasting life.*"

Notice that the word *whosoever* is underlined here. That is because I want to emphasize that salvation is a choice. Let's look at another verse of Scripture. Ephesians 2:8 says, *"For that by grace are ye saved through faith."* This verse teaches us that salvation comes by grace through faith in Christ Jesus.

We already proved through God's Word that salvation is a choice that you alone must make. When you call upon Jesus Christ to save you, it is His grace that allows you to accept Him by faith. Common reasoning then teaches us that (1) if salvation is a choice, (2) if it takes God's grace to save us, and (3) if His saving grace is not forced upon you (4) then you must reach out to Him and accept it.

Now, read the latter part of Ephesians 2:8: *"it is the gift of God."* No one forces a gift upon you. It must be received willingly.

Now, doesn't it stand to reason that, if saving grace is your choice to accept or reject, all other grace is your choice to accept or reject as well. This misunderstanding of God causes many people to stumble during tough times, trials, or personal storms in their lives.

It's not uncommon to grow weak in our faith when we are going through a trial. I already explained how the devil tricks us and lies to us during these times. Because we get disillusioned and are being tormented inside, it's easy to lose our focus to the truth. Before we know it we begin to blame God for not being with us during our most needed moment.

We start wondering why His grace is not carrying us through. The real truth though is that God is there, wanting to give us that grace which will carry us through. So often though, we have allowed ourselves to build up bitterness, resentment, and anger toward others, and even toward God Himself. These emotions of fear and hostility will not allow us to receive the grace which God is wanting to give us.

Even yet, God's unseen grace is still carrying us through that trial. Unless we get past those things which are hindering our spiritual walk, God's healing grace cannot do the work He wants to do in our lives. Again, just as God will not force His saving grace upon you, neither will He force any other part of His grace upon you.

God's grace takes away all our pain and hurt.

The last misconception deals with the suffering Christian. I'm talking about those individuals who are experiencing pain and hurt in their hearts and spirits.

As believers, it's hard to honestly fathom the idea of living our Christian lives while suffering the hurt and pain of a previous or present trial that we may be going through. As a matter of fact, when we experience this kind of pain, it's not uncommon to believe that God has let us down. We may even begin to doubt that the promises of His Word really are true.

Someone once said that it's often easier for non-Christians to get past tragedy in their lives because they really don't expect anything from God in the first place. As Christians, though, we live with the expectation that God won't allow us to suffer or experience any long-term pain in this life.

I certainly am not trying to confuse anyone, here, or bring controversy to the Bible, which has already been attacked repeatedly by scoffers and naysayers. The truth is, though, that it's necessary to understand the truths and promises of God's Word in their intended context. Allow me to give some examples of what I am talking about. I want you to carefully read the following verses of Scripture from God's Holy Word.

We are troubled on every side, yet not distressed;
we are perplexed, but not in despair. Persecuted,

but not forsaken; cast down, but not destroyed. (2
Corinthians 4:8,9)

*Who shall separate us from the love of Christ? Shall
tribulation, or distress, or persecution, or famine, or
nakedness, or peril, or sword?*
*As it is written, For thy sake we are killed all the day
long; we are accounted as sheep for the slaughter.
Nay, in all these things we are more than conquerors
through him that loved us. For I am persuaded, that
neither death, nor life, nor angels, nor principalities,
nor powers, nor things present, nor things to come,
Nor height, nor depth, nor any other creature, shall
be able to separate us from the love of God, which is
in Christ Jesus our Lord.* (Romans 8:35-39)

*When thou passest through the waters, I will be with
thee; and through the rivers, they shall not overflow
thee: when thou walkest through the fire, thou shalt
not be burned; neither shall the flame kindle thee.*
(Isaiah 43:2)

We sometimes accuse God of not keeping His promises
to us, when in fact He never promised there would not be
tough times that we would go through. Look at 2 Corinthians
4:8,9, again. We actually see that God told us that we would
face difficult times in our lives. We also see the power of
God's sustaining grace, which is able to carry us through
any situation or circumstance. These verses tell us that life
may bring trouble on every side, but grace will keep us from
being distressed. We may find ourselves perplexed, but grace
rescues us from despair. Though we may be persecuted,
grace assures us that God will not forsake us. The enemy of
our soul may cast us down, but grace will not allow him to
destroy us.

What a powerful example we are given here in God's Word of what it means to be a Christian. God gives us no misleading promises that, as a Christian, we will never face difficult times. What He does promise is that, when those tough times do come, grace will see us through. Thank God for sustaining grace!

Again, consider what the apostle Paul writes in Romans 8:35-39 concerning the trials of life. Verse 35 tells us of several obstacles which may come our way in this life, but verses 38 and 39 implore to us that, by God's sustaining grace, neither these things nor any other thing can separate us from the love of God, which is in Christ Jesus our Lord.

Finally, Isaiah 43:2 makes no apologies for speaking the truth of what to expect as a follower of God. This verse assures us that at some point in your life you will pass through the deep waters, and there will be times when you will feel the heat of the fire as you are in the midst of its blazing fury. Once again, though, there is God's sustaining grace which will not allow the waters to overflow you nor the fire to burn you.

I hope you have gotten the full picture of what I am trying to say here concerning the misconceptions about God and grace.

Once again, I must stress that God never promised we wouldn't go through the fire. What He did promise was that He would be there with us. Only when we begin to understand the truth of that promise can we fully be open to His grace which will carry us through.

I believe that sometimes the pain and hurt we experience in this life is intensified by our misconception of God's promises to us. When we add to our suffering the thought that God has let us down as well, the healing that we are so desperately in need of cannot come. That is because we have not allowed ourselves to be in the correct spiritual position in order to receive that healing. Do you remember what I said earlier about God not forcing grace upon us? If we are blaming God for our problems, how then are we spiritually able to receive His healing? The answer: we aren't.

Chapter 12

The Key to Spiritual Healing

For if ye forgive men their trespasses, your heavenly
Father will also forgive you.
(Matthew 6:14)

Though my knowledge is still limited, to say the least, I have learned much more about grace these past few years than what I ever knew previously. I have learned about grace I never knew. God has taught me much about spiritual healing and sustaining grace that I pray will allow me to minister to others.

I no longer have any false misconceptions about the pain and hurt that we experience as Christians. I realize that I am going to have to tread deep waters from time to time. I understand that there are going to be times when the fiery trials of life will encompass me. I have learned, though, that truly God is with me. Grace will not allow the waters to overflow me nor the fires to burn me.

I now understand that there is a certain amount of pain that I must endure in this life just because I am a Christian. Do you think that sounds unfair? Please don't tell that to God who gave His perfect and sinless Son to die for you and me. There is a logical reason and purpose for the pain, hurt, and suffering that we experience here.

As long as I live in this earthly tabernacle I know that I am never going to completely get over the losses of Kristy and Dani. Though God's grace is sufficient and will sustain me, I understand that there is pain associated with their departures, which will always remain with me. Even though I know they are both now safe in the arms of God, I still have days when I am blinded by my tears because I miss them so much. "So, Terry," you may be wondering, "how is there logic and reasoning to the idea that it's all right to experience that kind of pain in your life? Wouldn't it be better if God erased all that pain completely?"

By God's grace, I have come to understand the advantages of going through trials and tribulations in this life. There are at least four benefits we gain from suffering for Christ:

1. Our endurance of trials brings glory to God.
2. Our suffering provides an opportunity for our faith to grow, which results in spiritual maturity.
3. We learn through our suffering that we can trust in God to see us through.
4. The pain and suffering we endure provides opportunities to minister to others.

Of course, our greatest duty as a Christian is to bring glory to God, so that is the first and greatest benefit of suffering for Christ. A close second, though, is that our suffering provides opportunities to minister to others.

I have come to learn that my greatest purpose in this life is not to please the desires of my own fleshly nature. Rather, my greatest mission is to give God the praise of which He is worthy through bringing glory and honor to His Son, Jesus Christ, my Lord and Savior.

The greatest way we can bring glory and honor to Jesus is to tell others about Him. There is no extent to which God will not go to reach a lost soul. Our Heavenly Father will use any means necessary to reach a lost and dying world. The trials, tragedies, and testimonies of believers can be used not only to reach a lost world but also to help minister to other hurting Christians. If we will allow God to use us, we can witness to others about how our God will not let us down. God will use each one of us who will submit our lives to Him, to show that His many promises are true and that we can trust Him in every circumstance and situation.

If God took all my pain away, how would I ever be able to share someone else's pain who is going through the same loss which I knew to be so devastating? If God removed that pain from my life completely then I'm certain that I would eventually forget just how terrible that pain really was. Because I do still hurt, though, I can honestly sympathize with someone else who is also experiencing this same pain. Because I have been in the same shoes they are now walking in, I can share that burden with them. This is how God can and wants to use us in ministry, if we will only give Him complete reign in our lives.

It took me many months to come to the place where I felt that I could help others. If I was going to be honest, I guess I would have to admit that for too long I was just too absorbed in my own struggles and battles to be of any significant help to anyone else.

Everyone's healing process is different. Maybe you have been in my shoes and were able to move on much quicker than I. The healing time and process between Steph and myself has not been the same, even though we both experienced the same tragedy and pain. God created each one of us in His own unique way. Our personalities, varied backgrounds, and many other factors can all determine how we cope with personal trials, storms, and tragedies in our lives.

No one has the right to say when it's time for you to move on if they have not walked in your shoes.

I want God to use me and what I have been through to help others. I know that it was His will to take Kristy and Dani at their tender, young ages. It doesn't matter that I don't understand why. That is His business. As much as I still feel the pain of their absence in my life, I can now honestly say that I never want God to take the memory of that pain away from me. Because of the pain I experienced from Kristy and Dani's deaths, I know that God can, and will, use me to encourage and help others who are lost and hurting. The sustaining grace that He provides for me abounds much more than the pain I feel. Again, I can't explain this kind of grace. You just have to take my word for it. Who is intelligent enough, wise enough, or blessed with enough knowledge to explain the workings of our Heavenly Father and His amazing grace? Certainly not I. I can only testify of the truth of Paul's words from our Lord in 2 Corinthians 12:9: "*My grace is sufficient for thee: for my strength is made perfect in weakness.*"

There is one more important truth that must be discussed concerning grace and spiritual healing. Quite honestly though, this may be the most important truth of all to grasp hold of. When I came to the knowledge of this truth, it was the start of my healing that I was so desperately in need of.

This truth that I'm talking about is found in one simple, yet gigantic word, as far as spiritual healing and restitution are concerned. That word is "forgiveness." I have come to learn that the most integral part of any healing process starts with forgiveness.

Forgiveness is the key that unlocks all of man's problems. Forgiveness is the main ingredient to getting past all of our problems—past, present, or future.

We had to be forgiven by God before we could be saved. Let's look at a few verses of Scripture which explain more clearly the necessity of forgiveness.

First, there is a call to repentance to the sinner:

Repent ye therefore, and be converted, that your sins may be blotted out, when the times of refreshing shall come from the presence of the Lord. (Acts 3:19)

When we sincerely come to the Lord and ask His forgiveness, He is always faithful to forgive us.

In whom we have redemption through his blood, the forgiveness of sins, according to the riches of his grace. (Ephesians 1:7)

If we confess our sins, he is faithful and just to forgive us our sins, and to cleanse us from all unrighteousness. (1 John 1:9)

Forgiveness is not intended to be a characteristic of God alone. It should be a characteristic of those who belong to Him as well. The Holy Bible teaches us that if we expect to receive forgiveness from God then we must also be willing to forgive others.

And when ye stand praying, forgive, if ye have ought against any: that your Father also which is in heaven may forgive you your trespasses. (Mark 11:25)

And be ye kind one to another, tenderhearted, forgiving one another, even as God for Christ's sake hath forgiven you. (Ephesians 4:32)

*Forbearing one another, and forgiving one another,
if any man have a quarrel against any: even as Christ
forgave you, so also do ye.* (Colossians 3:13)

Forgiveness is that key that unlocks everything holding us in bondage. Forgiveness tears down fear, anxiety, depression, anger, bitterness, hatred, and everything else that may hinder us from enjoying our salvation to its fullest extent. Forgiveness will restore the peace in our hearts and the joy of serving the Lord that we are supposed to have as Christians. Without a heart of forgiveness, it is impossible to live the abundant life that Christ talked about in John 10:10.

In fact, if we refuse to forgive others, Jesus said that our Heavenly Father will not forgive us.

*But if ye do not forgive, neither will your Father
which is in heaven forgive your trespasses.* (Mark
11:26)

As we go through the trials and storms of life, it is often hard to understand why these things are happening to us. Satan feasts on these opportunities to whisper in our ear and weaken our faith. As a result of this, it is not uncommon to even become angry with God.

There now even comes a point in our lives where we must also be willing to forgive God. (Before you turn me off after that statement, please continue to read on.) I know as well as you that God has never done anything that requires forgiveness. However, when we are dealing with someone who has deep rooted resentment, it becomes essential to meet with them on common ground which they can understand. That individual is already struggling with understanding why God has allowed them to experience such pain. To expect them to just "get over it" by saying that God has a right to do whatever He chooses is almost asinine to think that's an answer that will suffice.

So, what do you say to someone who is bitter and angry at God for some reason? How can that person ever get past the pain and hurt that they have endured and renew their relationship with their Heavenly Father?

We already said that "forgiveness" is the key that unlocks all of life's problems. To forgive someone whom we feel has wronged us is essential before we can move on spiritually. As strange as it may sound, sometimes it becomes necessary for us to even forgive God for the things we have blamed Him for. Please don't misunderstand what I am saying here. I realize that God is the One who must forgive us, and it almost sounds ridiculous, if not blasphemous to suggest that God has made a mistake and now needs our approval to be God again. The truth is, though, that this kind of anger and bitterness must be dealt with in sincerity and honesty from a humble heart. At these times we must come to God and absolve any ill feelings that we have had with Him. Then we ask His forgiveness for our lack of faith. This is called reconciliation, and it is the only way that we can ever move on in our personal relationship with God.

God already knows your thoughts. Don't think you are taking Him by surprise with your words of honesty. He has been patiently waiting for you to open your heart to Him. He wants nothing more than to restore that torn relationship with you. Remember, it was not God who turned away. We are the ones who always stray from His presence, but every time, He is waiting with open arms of forgiveness. All we have to do is ask.

It took God's forgiveness to heal us of our disease of sin. It sometimes takes our forgiving God in order to start healing from our wounds and hurts.

That brings us to our final point on forgiveness. Because we have struggled for so long with bitterness toward God, the old devil will now bring feelings of guilt into our minds of how we unjustly accused God of wronging us. This guilt can sometimes become so overwhelming that we now feel unworthy to be forgiven of God. I already warned you how Satan never gives up. When one door closes, he looks for another one to sneak in. At this time it becomes essential to bury yourselves in the promises of God and remember what He said you are in Christ Jesus. You must remember that He has cast your sins away as far as the east is from the west, never to be remembered again. You are complete in Christ Jesus, and nothing can separate you from the love of God. Satan needs to be reminded of that on a regular basis. You now belong to God, and Satan cannot take what belongs to Him.

Now therefore ye are no more strangers and foreigners, but fellow citizens with the saints, and of the household of God. (Ephesians 2:19)

But as many as received him, to them gave he power to become the sons of God, even to them that believe on his name. (John 1:12)

See how God looks at you. This is the way you must now perceive your own self in Christ Jesus. It is nothing you have done. Rather, it is everything He has done. When you come to this place in God, your healing process can begin. You will now begin to experience the grace of God in your life as you never imagined you could.

I want to clarify something before closing this chapter. I have talked a lot about trials, pain, and suffering for Christ. I don't want you to have the impression that pain endured for Christ never ceases. Time truly is a wonderful healer.

In mine and Stephanie's case, we know that the pain of losing Kristy and Dani will never completely go away, but we have learned how grace eases that pain as we submit our lives to the Lord for His use.

Let me give you an analogy to further express this crucial point. Someone may receive a nasty cut on their body. Though the pain of that cut may eventually cease to exist, the scar is a constant reminder of what once happened. Though our pain is not what it once was, there are scars that will remain forever. Those scars are a reminder of just how much we miss and loved Kristy and Dani. Whenever Steph and I hear of someone losing a loved one, we are instantly reminded of our own pain that we endured from losing our daughter and granddaughter. It doesn't take long for that pain that we know so well to resurface in our hearts. That is when God is able to use us to minister to others who are hurting. I thank Him that my pain and suffering can be used for His glory.

I think it is certainly worth mentioning that the greatest scars of all were endured by our Lord Himself, Jesus Christ. Those nail prints in His hands and feet will remain there for all eternity. They will be a constant reminder of what our Savior did for you and me.

When you consider how the perfect and sinless Son of God endured the shame, agony, and pain of a cruel cross so that we may inherit eternal life, we should all be reminded that any suffering we go through in this life is not comparable to what He endured.

But he was wounded for our transgressions, he was bruised for our iniquities: the chastisement of our peace was upon him; and with his stripes we are healed. (Isaiah 53:5)

Thank you Jesus, for suffering and dying for my sins. By your stripes, Lord, I am eternally healed.

Chapter 13

Moving On

Fear thou not; for I am with thee: be not dismayed;
for I am thy God: I will strengthen thee; yea, I will
help thee; yea, I will uphold thee with the right
hand of my righteousness.
(Isaiah 41:10)

I have several reasons for writing this book. First and foremost, of course, is to bring glory and honor to Jesus Christ, my Lord and Savior. Next, I have written "Grace I Never Knew" so that my grandchildren will always know how wonderful their mother was and for them to understand the wonderful working grace of God that sustains us through the trials of life. Last, but certainly not least, I want to show others that there is hope when they may think that all hope is gone and that God has forgotten about you.

The tests and trials of life are inevitable. Someone once said, "There are three kinds of people: those who have gone through problems, those who are going through problems, those who will eventually go through problems." Which one of these people describes you, my friend?

If you are going through something that has shattered your faith and left you wondering if God even really cares anymore then I have good news for you. God does care about you. He loves you so much that He wants to be in every part of your life. There is light at the end of the tunnel, and that light is Jesus Christ.

Everyone's trials and storms in life are different. God is the Master Designer, and He created each one of us in His own unique way. Because we all have different traits, characteristics, and personalities, it only stands to reason that each one of us will come through the trials of life differently.

The Lord Jesus Christ has a specific plan for your life. I want to encourage you to seek His will for your life. Sometimes we tend to deviate or stray from His plans (Jonah is a good example). It then becomes necessary for the Lord to take other routes to get our attention. All the while, though, He is patiently watching and waiting for us to come on board with Him.

As I look back, I now realize that God wanted to use me in the ministry long before I accepted His call on my life. Only ten months after accepting that call, my daughter died as a result of that tragic car wreck. I spent the next two-plus years searching for direction. Much of that time has been spent struggling with the pain of losing Kristy and Dani. While I was struggling and searching, God was patiently waiting, while His grace has been healing and sustaining this unworthy servant.

In all honesty, for several months after Kristy and Dani's deaths, I didn't care about the ministry. I told God that I had no desire, and I even begged Him to release me from that calling. Though He has been patient with me, He has never allowed me to feel at ease with giving up the ministry. Sure, I could walk away from His will for my life and still be saved. My salvation doesn't depend upon my works or even my personal ministry for that matter. My salvation is dependant upon the fact that I have accepted the Lord Jesus Christ as my Savior, admitting that I am a sinner, and confessing that His precious blood has covered my sins. By grace, I am saved through faith in Christ Jesus.

Herein lies the problem, though. I may walk away from God's call upon my life, but because I am now walking according to my will, and not His, I am headed for a life of misery. One doesn't walk away from God's plans and not feel the effects from it. I am speaking from personal experience. I spent several months after Kristy and Dani's deaths doing ministry in the flesh. For the longest time my heart just wasn't in it. I may have been performing the call on the outside, but I was running from God on the inside. During those months of running I was a very miserable person. I think I know a little how old Jonah must have felt as he was lying in the belly of that great fish. You eventually come to the place where you realize that, as hard as ministry may be at times, it sure beats fighting against God.

I have had much to learn, and God has had a captive audience with me. God trapped me in a corner, and when I realized that I had nowhere else to turn, there He was saying, "Now, my son, let's do it my way, and see how I will bless you." As I have learned to be submissive to God and His grace, I have once again began to experience the peace and joy of serving the Lord that had previously eluded me. My relationship with my Heavenly Father is better now than at any other time in my Christian life. I have learned to trust Him as my faith has grown. I have become more discerning of His voice. I know that He has a specific plan for my life, and with all my heart I want to pursue and fulfill His perfect will for Stephanie and myself. What I have to be careful of is to not become overzealous and get ahead of God, which we all tend to do at times.

Steph and I have gone through more changes over these past two-plus years than all of the other years combined in our married lives. Matt is now married again, and we are happy to say that he is doing very well. He and his new wife, Lisa, have their hands full. Under their roof, of course, is Gabriel, Terryann, and Aaryn. Lisa has two daughters, Noel and Grace, and they have been recently blessed with a new son of their own, Ethan Nathaniel Woodcox.

As happy as we are for Matt, it wasn't easy watching him remarry. That is nothing against Lisa. We love her dearly, and they have all of our support. I think you can probably understand what I'm saying. As much as we love Lisa and her daughters, it's been hard watching someone else move into the same house two doors down where our daughter used to live. That is just as much a fact and reality of life as it was that Matt had to move on with his life.

With Matt's new expanded family it became essential for them to move into a bigger house. We had to make the adjustment of not seeing Gabe, Terryann, and Aaryn as often as we were once accustomed. Gabe, Terryann, and Aaryn mean more to Steph and me than life itself. We still see Kristy in each one of their lives, and together they are a constant reminder of our little Dani.

We have had to make many adjustments to our lives. As hard as it has sometimes been, I am more confident today than ever before that we are getting there. Each passing day we are learning more and more to trust in God to lead and direct our paths.

Steph and I started attending the Heritage Free Will Baptist Church in August 2002. We took membership in November of that year and immediately became actively involved in the church. I think that is the way it's supposed to be.

I started teaching an adult Sunday School class, became active in the men's group, and tried to be a support and help in any way I could to Pastor Tim and the church. In July

2004 I accepted God's call on my life to go into the ministry. In March 2005 I became a licensed minister.

Meanwhile, my ministry duties grew as I became the Master's Men's Chaplain in our men's group, as well as being the Executive Secretary in our denominational conference. I'm not saying all this to show how much I was doing or was involved in. My point is that I was actively involved in ministry. So, you might be wondering, "Isn't that enough to do? Why are you seeking God's will for what you are now supposed to be doing?" My answer to that is, "It's not about how much you are doing." The question should always be, "Am I doing what God has called me to do?"

I have to be honest with you. I have always wanted to stay at Heritage. I thought that is where God sent me, and I supposed that was where I would always minister. About the beginning of 2007, though, I began to feel as though God had other plans. Here is a good lesson to always remember. Even if you think God may be moving you, continue to minister where you are until you have definite directions where you should be.

I talked about being overzealous as we are waiting on God's will to transpire in our lives. That is exactly what happened to me. I felt that God was going to move me, but instead of allowing Him to do it, I walked though a door that He wasn't opening.

One day I stopped in to talk with Pastor Tim. I told him that I believed God was leading me to another church that was going to provide an opportunity for possible full-time ministry. I was so excited, and I just knew that God was in the picture. No one could have convinced me otherwise, even though Pastor Tim tried.

Well, I left Heritage and was only gone about two weeks when I realized that I missed it. I wasn't in God's will and both Steph and I were very miserable. I now had two choices and neither one was very appealing at the time. We could just stay at our new church and know that we weren't in God's will, or we could swallow our pride and go back to Heritage, admitting that we got ahead of God. Actually, there was no choice to be made. I knew that I had been miserable enough these past several months without adding to my misery by being out of God's will. I must once again refer back to Jonah and this poor man's dismal situation. The last thing I wanted was to be vomited up on dry land (Jonah 2:10).

After several more weeks of praying for direction, I was continually reminded of what my good friend Gary Whaley told me when he was counseling to me. Pastor Gary said to me, "Terry, if you will allow God, He can and will build your ministry upon Kristy's death." Those words echoed in heart and spirit day and night.

Several more weeks passed when Steph and I once again felt God's leading to leave our church at Heritage. God was leading us to the Canaan Land Free Will Baptist Church in Grove City, OH. We were at Canaan Land for only two weeks when a lady introduced herself to Steph and shared that she had lost her son in an automobile accident just five months prior to Kristy and Dani's deaths. She just needed to talk with someone else who knew her pain. I left Canaan Land that morning understanding more fully the words that Pastor Gary Whaley shared with me several months earlier.

Though I am a minister of God's Word, I know that mine and Steph's greatest ministry is reaching out to others who are lost and hurting. Some ministers only want to preach, but my greatest joy is experienced when I can help lead a lost person to Jesus Christ or when I can share a word that will bring hope and encouragement to someone who may be torn in their spirit from overwhelming grief and pain.

Each day brings new trials, struggles, and challenges. I know there are still days when I fail to reach the plateau that God has in mind for me. I still face the onslaught of the enemy whose desire is to sift me as wheat so that I will be of no use to the work of God's kingdom.

Thank God, though, I have learned to lean upon grace when I didn't know what to do next. Because God has brought me safely, thus far, I know that He will see me through to the end. Philippians 1:6 has become one of my favorite verses in all the Bible: "*Being confident of this very thing, that he which hath begun a good work in you will perform it until the day of Jesus Christ.*" I trust in my Heavenly Father. He knows what is best for me. I thank Him for His faithfulness, that He has never failed me, left me, nor forsaken me. I am honored and privileged to be counted as a servant for the Lord Jesus Christ.

As Stephanie and I continue to seek God's will and direction for our lives, I beg you to please keep us in your prayers. As you know by now, the road is not always smooth sailing. None of us knows what tomorrow holds, but praise God we know who holds tomorrow. Please pray that we may reach lost and hurting souls for the Lord. Pray that we will stay strong in our faith. Pray that we will not grow weary in well doing (Galatians 6:9). Most of all, please pray that in all that we do it will bring glory and honor to the name of Jesus Christ, who is worthy of all praise!

****

This book is about grace. God's grace works in many different ways. I have been a recipient of the supernatural working of grace. I'm talking about grace that touches the spirit and heart of man that cannot be explained or understood.

I have come to learn that God's grace is also extended to us through people. God uses people to touch our lives in ways that make a difference. I want to tell you about some people who have impacted the lives of this family, and I'm sure they didn't even realize it. What these individuals did, they did from a kind and caring heart. I know they didn't do them for the accolades, but I would be remiss if I didn't recognize certain ones for the way they showed their love and support to this family these past few years.

I'm not sure that we always realize how one unnoticed and small act of kindness can make such a huge difference in the life of another individual. I want to thank the following people for allowing God's grace to work through them to touch Steph's and my life.

Erin Flanagan - When God's people are going through personal trials or tragedy He graciously surrounds us with others to help comfort us, even when we don't realize it. Erin was someone that the Lord blessed us with. Erin was one of Kristy's nurses at the Grant Hospital trauma unit. She was more than a nurse that week, though. She was a godsend that Steph and I needed during those intense and emotional few days. Erin would talk to us about Kristy as though she knew her. She asked us questions about her and the kids. You could tell that she genuinely cared about what we were going through. The special attention that Erin provided and the little things she did for us made a difference those few days we were there, to say the least. That young lady went beyond her call of duty in being a nurse. On Friday evening of that week, she came into the room with a pan of water, shampoo, a hair brush, and a comb. She asked Steph if she would like to help her wash Kristy's hair and brush it out. We later discovered that wasn't a requirement in her job description. Erin did that on her own. That act of care and concern touched Steph more than Erin will ever know. Erin's greatness as a nurse is only superseded by her greatness as a person. To Steph and me, she was our angel.

Jeff and Cari Spence - Jeff and Cari are the funeral directors of the Spence—Miller Funeral Home in Grove City, where we live. Spence—Miller handled all the funeral arrangements for Kristy and Dani. Since Dani died at the accident, we were waiting as long as possible to have her funeral in hopes that Kristy would live. I couldn't bear the thought of her coming out of a coma and learning that Dani had died and had already been buried. I knew that would have been terribly hard for her. Weeks after their funerals, Pastor Tim told me something that touched my heart immensely. Cari was torn by the thought of that little girl being in that cold dark room all alone. She actually took one of her own daughter's baby dolls and laid it beside of Dani. Cari will never know how much that touched mine and Stephanie's hearts. It is just another example of the love and compassion that was shown toward our grieving family. I will never forget that small, yet life-altering act of compassion displayed by Jeff and Cari.

Jerry Stewart - Jerry goes to the Heritage Free Will Baptist Church. If you want to see the transformation that takes place in one's life after meeting Jesus Christ, go talk to Jerry. Before he met Jesus, Jerry led a very rough life. He was into alcohol, drugs, and other things that were destroying his life. Jerry used to be a bar bouncer, if that tells you anything. After Jerry accepted Christ into his heart, his life did a complete turnaround. That is what "repent" means—to turn—and that is exactly what Jerry did. Though Jerry is young in the Lord, he is the epitome of what being a Christian is all about. Ecclesiastes 9:10 says; *"Whatsoever thy hand findeth to do, do it with thy might."* That Scripture describes Jerry. He does all that he knows to do for the work of the Lord. Jerry is usually the first one at the church when the doors open. He greets people, hands out bulletins, cuts grass, plows snow, and anything else that he can find to do.

Jerry puts a lot of us, who have been serving the Lord for years, to shame in his willingness to work for God.

Matt was laid up for awhile himself after the wreck and was busy taking care of those important matters that needed his attention. Jerry took it upon himself to care for Matt's yard the rest of that summer. He did the mowing, weed-eating and anything else that needed kept up around the house. He even volunteered to do my yard, but I assured him I was fine. God has a special reward for people like Jerry Stewart, who places the welfare of others ahead of himself. I'm proud to call Jerry my friend and my brother-in-Christ.

Pam Means - To put it plain and simple, Pam and her husband Patrick are just good people. They are wonderful Christians whom I've known for years. What makes people like Patrick and Pam so special is the fact that they live what they profess. Here is another example of someone "*doing whatsoever their hand findeth to do.*" Pam cleans houses to supplement her and Patrick's income. Realizing that Matt now had his hands full while trying to work and raise three children, Pam volunteered to come in once a week and clean their house for an entire year. I'm not talking about just picking up a few toys and sweeping a rug or two. Pam cleaned that house as if it were her own, and when she left it, was immaculate. Pam's act of kindness will never be forgotten.

Bill and Vickie Fitzpatrick - The list just goes on and on. Bill and Vickie attend the Heritage Free Will Baptist Church. I have known Bill and Vickie for several years and like Patrick and Pam Means, I can testify to their genuine love for God and their desire to please Him in all that they do. When all of our lives got back to some form of normalcy (as much as was possible), there often arose the need for someone to watch Gabe and Terryann after school let out.

Vickie volunteered to watch the kids as much as we needed her. There were many days that I would pick them up after school and take them straight to Vickie's house as I was on my way to work. Bill and Vickie were such a blessing to us for all that they did to help in this area. It relieved a lot of stress and tension in knowing that we always had somewhere safe for the kids to go. The world needs more people like Bill and Vickie Fitzpatrick.

Linda Rehmert - Mrs. Rehmert taught kindergarten at the J.C. Sommer Elementary School where Gabe and Terryann went. She had Gabe in her class the year before Kristy died, and Terryann would be in her class the next school year of 2005-06. On the last day of school in 2005, Mrs. Rehmert asked Steph and me if we could come to her room for a few minutes. The teachers and staff at J.C. Sommer had bought Gabe and Terryann toys, books, games, crayons and markers so they could stay occupied during that summer after their mommy had died. Here is another example of God using ordinary people to exhibit His grace.

Mrs. Rehmert retired after the 2006-07 school year. She taught kindergarten for thirty-five years at the same school. J.C. Sommer will miss her immensely. Like Erin, Mrs. Rehmert went far beyond her job—she was much more than a teacher. She was an angel who made a difference in someone's life who desperately needed a touch. Terryann still talks about Mrs. Rehmert. Every school needs a Mrs. Rehmert.

The Eberhard Family - Chris, Cheri, and Logan Eberhard are my next-door neighbors. Chris is a highly respected police officer in Grove City. His wife, Cheri, and their son Logan have been instrumental in our lives as well, though they probably didn't even realize it. I told Jerry Stewart not to worry about mowing my grass and that I could take care of it. That summer I usually didn't get a chance to take care of it anyway. Chris took it upon himself to mow my lawn as he was mowing his own. Chris and Cheri's friendly and smiling faces are always a pick-me-up, even on our lowest day.

Then there is Logan. Logan is three years older than Gabe. Gabe thinks the sun rises and sets on Logan. Logan kind of adopted Gabe as his little brother. Those two have spent hours and hours playing together, and Logan will never know how much he means to Gabe. Chris has been so good to include Gabe in his activities. He has taken them to football games, to the water park, bike riding, and many other things that have made a difference in Gabe's life. I can't thank Chris, Cheri, and Logan enough for the ways that they made Gabe feel so special. Everyone should be fortunate enough to have neighbors like Chris, Cheri, and Logan.

Maxine Damron - The last person I want to mention, but certainly not least, is Maxine Damron. Maxine is a widower at our church. She has been a stronghold in mine and Stephanie's lives. We have lost count of the number of cards and letters this sweet lady has showered us with. She continually lets us know that she is praying for us. Maxine has been such a blessing to us and a constant source of encouragement. I thank God for Maxine Damron.

The people I have just mentioned should never be taken for granted. Their acts of kindness and generosity have literally changed the lives of other people, including my own. I cannot put into words how much each one of them means to me. I only hope that, somehow, someway I can be as much a blessing to them as they have been to me. I love and respect each one of them. I pray that God will bless each one of them immensely with His richest and deepest blessings. They are certainly deserving of it.

It's just not possible to mention every person who has touched mine and Stephanie's lives these past few years. There are far too many to name individually. I only hope and pray that I can be as much a blessing to those who have supported us as they have been to Stephanie and me.

Chapter 14

God's Plan of Salvation

But God commendeth his love toward us, in that,
while we were yet sinners, Christ died for us.
(Romans 5:8)

In the Old Testament the chief purpose of altars was for the offering of sacrifices and the burning of incense. The altar was the place of sacrifice where God was propitiated and where man was pardoned and sanctified. Today, the altar is a place where men and women can recognize that Jesus Christ willingly died for their sins. When any individual confesses this recognition of what Christ has done for them, they can then ask the Lord to forgive their sins. The altar then becomes a spiritual symbol of that individual sacrificing their old life for a new life in Christ Jesus.

I have always said that no message is complete without an altar call, which is an invitation for us to symbolically sacrifice ourselves to God's will. Any preacher who prepares a sermon, prays over it, preaches it, and then fails to give an altar call has wasted a precious and valuable opportunity. Every message that is preached should provide the opportunity for lost souls to give their heart to Jesus Christ.

I feel the same way about this book. It would not be complete without sharing the gospel of the Lord Jesus Christ and inviting you to accept Him as your personal Savior. The intentions of "Grace I Never Knew" are many. I certainly hope and pray that its message has clearly and precisely conveyed the hope, strength, power, and magnitude of God's grace. Even more importantly, though, I pray that the Lord will use this book to reach lost and hurting people.

I remember reading something one time that always stuck with me. Someone said that people often spend hundreds of hours planning for their retirement years, but not a minute preparing for eternity.

Before you read any further I would ask you to ponder that statement for a moment if you will. People spend hundreds of hours planning for what averages out to be about fifteen more years of living on this earth, but they don't spend one minute giving thought to where they will spend eternity.

I wonder if you can honestly grasp the mind-boggling thought of eternity. I heard a minister one time give his description of how long eternity was. Think about it as I share what he said.

Let's suppose you drained all the oceans and seas upon the face of the earth until there only remained the sand on the bottom. You took a bird and had it fly one grain of sand at a time to the moon. Let's suppose it took the bird a thousand years to get to the moon, and a thousand years to get back. Think about the countless thousands upon thousands of years we are talking about here, in order to get every last grain of sand from every ocean, sea, and river throughout the whole earth.

After those millions of years have passed by and the bird's task is completed, he must then start on the grains of sand in all the deserts of the earth. You are talking about millions of more years that must pass by.

Finally, after the bird has carried away every last grain of sand on this earth to the moon, ETERNITY has only begun!

This little story probably doesn't even begin to faze some people, but it should. It should especially get your attention if you aren't sure where you will spend eternity. Friend, you are going to live forever in one of two places, either heaven or hell.

I realize this is not a popular topic to talk about. No one likes to think about burning forever in a lake of fire, as described in Revelation 20:14,15. Many people seem to think if they just ignore it, it won't really happen. Please don't let Satan trick you into believing a lie my friend. Hell is every much as real as heaven is.

I was talking to a man I worked with one time. He was explaining to me how ridiculous I was for wasting my time going to church and serving a God who didn't even really exist anyway. He said that I should be out doing things that were worthwhile. In his words, "Terry, you only live once. So, you better live it up now and get everything you can, because once you die, it's over."

I explained to this man that what he didn't understand was that I was happy going to church and serving the Lord. I had no desire to be involved in the worldly activities that he spoke of. I didn't need those things to make my life complete.

I wanted to get right down to where the rubber meets the road with this fellow, so I said to him, "Just suppose you are right and I am wrong. What if we do just die and that's it? There is no God, no heaven, or no hell. What have I lost?"

He said that I would have thrown my whole life away chasing after something that wasn't true when I could have been doing more worthwhile things. I told him I could live with that, because in all honesty, I was already having the time of my life anyway. It was hard for him to believe that I could really be as happy as I claimed to be. It just goes to prove that there really is a peace with serving the Lord that surpasses the understanding of men (Philippians 4:7).

I then asked him a question that I also want you to consider if you haven't asked Christ to be Lord of your life. "But, what if I am right and you are wrong?" I asked him. "What if there is a hell where you will remain throughout eternity? Then, what have you lost?" I went on to explain to him that he will have lost everything, and there will be no second chance. That fellow never said another word to me. He just walked away.

Hell is real, my friend. Sadly, though, by the time multitudes of people come to understand the reality of that awful place, it will be too late. I must ask you today, isn't the mere possibility of the existence of hell and spending eternity there at least worth looking into? If not for yourself, what about your children and loved ones? Can you bear the thought of any one of them being in such a place of torment forever and ever, with no hope of an end? These are questions that should not be taken lightly.

Is there really a heaven?

God's Word assures us that heaven is real. It is a place of eternal beauty and splendor.

"...for God is in heaven..." (Ecclesiastes 5:2)

Do not I fill heaven and earth? saith the Lord? (Jeremiah 23:24)

Heaven is described as a glorious city, likened to pure gold and clear glass (Revelation 21:18). Its streets are made of gold (Revelation 21:21). Heaven will shine and be enlightened by God's glory (Revelation 22:5). The psalmist described it as a place of magnificent beauty (Psalm 50:2). Heaven is a place of everlasting joy (Psalm 16:11). God prepared heaven to last for all eternity (Psalm 23:6). No one will ever hunger or thirst again in that wonderful place (Revelation 7:16). There will be no more sickness in heaven (Revelation 22:5), and there will be no more tears, pain, nor death (Revelation 21:4).

In my Father's house are many mansions: if it were not so, I would have told you. I go to prepare a place for you. And if I go and prepare a place for you, I will come again, and receive you unto myself: that where I am, there ye may be also. (John 14:2,3)

Many skeptics claim that heaven doesn't exist, but that does not change the reality of it. During a blizzard one freezing, December night, a man was watching a television program. He saw people swimming and surfing in the 85 degree temperatures of Hawaii. He turned to a friend and said, "I don't believe a place such as that really exists." Well, we all know that Hawaii really does exist. So does heaven.

Is there a hell?

Just as sure as there is a place of splendor and beauty called heaven, there is a place of everlasting punishment called hell. The Bible tells us about a man who went there:

And it came to pass, that the beggar died, and was carried by the angels into Abraham's bosom: the rich man died and was also buried; And in hell he lift up his eyes, being in torments, and seeth Abraham afar

179

off, and Lazarus in his bosom. And he cried, Father Abraham, have mercy on me, and send Lazarus, that he may dip the tip of his finger in water, and cool my tongue; for I am tormented in this flame. (Luke 16:22-24)

It really is hard for our minds to comprehend a place this terrible. Hell is described as an "everlasting fire" (Matthew 25:41). It is called an "eternal fire" (Jude 7), and a "furnace of fire" (Matthew 13:42). In Revelation 20:10, hell is referred to as "the lake of fire and brimstone." Those who are there shall be tormented with fire and brimstone (Revelation 14:10).

Hell is a place of "outer darkness" (Matthew 8:12) and "blackness and darkness" (Jude 13). Hell's inhabitants endure "chains of darkness" (2 Peter 2:4) in a "bottomless pit" (Revelation 20:3)

Hell's inhabitants experience "weeping and gnashing of teeth" (Matthew 8:12), "everlasting destruction" (2 Thessalonians 1:9), and "...the smoke of their torment ascendeth up for ever and ever" (Revelation 14:11). The worst part of all is that hell's population increases every day, yet it is never full (Proverbs 27:20).

This terrible place of eternal torment was prepared for the devil and his angels (Matthew 25:41). Satan knows that hell awaits him as his final destiny (Isaiah 14:15; Revelation 20:10). So, too, will all those who reject Jesus Christ as the one and only way to reach heaven (2 Thessalonians 1:8).

It is impossible to comprehend the never-ending pain of that awful place called hell. To get just a small glimpse, imagine laying your hand on a red-hot stove. Though your hand would only remain there for a fraction of a second, you would no doubt scream out in pain. The agony of that pain would continue on until you received medical attention and the burn began to heal. Now imagine being unable to remove your hand from that stove. Even worse, visualize your whole body inside that burner with no way to escape, forever.

I understand this is not a pleasant picture to imagine. No one wants to ponder such a dreadful thing. My dear friend, even with this painted picture of the gruesomeness and ghastliness of hell, I still have not described what it will really be like. In describing the beauty of heaven, the apostle Paul wrote in 1 Corinthians 2:9, *eye hath not seen, nor ear heard, neither have entered into the heart of man, the things which God hath prepared for them that love him.* I don't think it's unrealistic to think that the same thing can be said of hell. Our finite minds cannot even begin to grasp the dreadfulness of that awful place. It is a destination that you want to avoid. Thanks to the love, mercy, and grace of our God, you can. Let's learn how.

How to become a Christian

The Bible tells us in 2 Peter 3:9 that it is God's will that none would perish, that He desires that all would come to repentance. I hope that in reading this chapter you have been convinced of your need to accept Jesus Christ as your personal Savior. You can be born-again right now by simply asking God to save you.

For whosoever shall call upon the name of the Lord shall be saved. (Romans 10:13)

Now, just pray to God in your own words. God isn't impressed with formal prayers. He wants you to talk to Him from your own heart. You must believe in your heart what you speak with your mouth.

That if thou shalt confess with thy mouth the Lord Jesus, and shalt believe in thine heart that God hath raised him from the dead, thou shalt be saved. For with the heart man believeth unto righteousness; and with the mouth confession is made unto salvation. (Romans 10:9,10)

Don't put it off. The Lord Jesus Christ is waiting for you.

Behold, I stand at the door and knock: if any man hear my voice, and open the door, I will come in to him, and will sup with him, and he with me. (Revelation 3:20)

If you would like to be saved and know that you are on your way to heaven, pray a prayer something like this from your heart:

Lord Jesus, I am a sinner and I am sorry for all of my sins that I have committed. I realize that I am lost in my present condition and on my way to hell. I know that the only way I can be saved is through faith in you. Thank you Jesus, for dying on the cross for me. Please forgive my sins and save me Lord. I now invite you to live in my heart. Right now Jesus, I trust you alone for my salvation. Amen.

Dear friend, if you prayed that prayer from your heart then you now belong to the family of God. You have just changed your eternal destination from one of doom to eternal bliss in Christ Jesus. You have just become a brand new person.

Therefore if any man be in Christ, he is a new creature: old things are passed away; behold, all things are become new. (2 Corinthians 5:17)

If you have made the decision to accept Christ as your personal Savior, I would like to know about it. Please contact me through my e-mail address listed at the beginning of this book. I want to pray for you. I would also like to send you some valuable information that will be helpful to you in your new journey as a Christian. I look forward to the day we can sit down together in heaven and fellowship with one another. We will have all eternity to do so.

Epilogue

And God shall wipe away all tears from their eyes;
and there shall be no more death, neither sorrow,
nor crying, neither shall there be any more pain: for
the former things are passed away.
(Revelation 21:4)

I have often said after Kristy and Dani's deaths that I wouldn't bring them back even if I could. More than a few people have looked at me in disbelief that I would say such a thing. One has to have a real understanding for the things of God to comprehend such a statement. Let me explain what I mean.

Do I wish the accident that took my daughter and granddaughter's lives had never happened? Of course I do. If it was God's desire to bring Kristy and Dani home to be with Him, am I happy that His will was fulfilled? Yes, I am. I know that may sound bizarre to some, and admittedly it took me a long time to come to the place in my life where I could say that. With the help of God's grace, though, I can now look at things in this life differently than I did before.

In thinking of the death of my own daughter I am reminded of the death of God's only Son. I am forced to ask myself the same question about Jesus that I did with Kristy. Do I wish that Jesus wouldn't have had to die on the cross? Yes, I do wish that He would not have had to endure the pain that He bore at Calvary. Am I glad that God's will was fulfilled in His death? Yes I am, because in His death I am saved, along with countless millions of others who have accepted His death as atonement for their sins.

It's almost a paradox when you think about it. I'm sorry that it happened, but I'm glad that it did. Certainly, we are not glad that Jesus had to die as He did, but we understand the necessity of His death. I can say the same thing about my daughter. I do not rejoice in her death, but I do trust my God. I can rejoice in the fact that, because He allowed it to happen He must have had a purpose for it. Just because I don't understand why gives me no legitimate reason to question God.

I am persuaded to believe that through Kristy's death others may come to the saving knowledge of Jesus Christ. It may be through the testimony of her life that she left behind which speaks to someone's heart who knew her so well. It may be through the testimony of her husband, children, or friends, who knew and loved her so much. I am certainly praying that mine and Stephanie's testimony of God's grace through our tragedy will lead lost and hurting souls to the saving knowledge of Jesus Christ. If even one person is saved through her death, was it worth it? Yes, it was. If you don't think so, ask that person ten million years from now as they are strolling down heaven's golden streets.

I knew my daughter well, and I can say with assurance that she would tell you the same thing. If Kristy would have thought her death would bring salvation to someone else then she would have been glad to do it. This is especially true of her friends and family members. Many times she and I talked about certain ones in our family and she would say, "Dad, what will it take for them to be saved?" I would say, "I don't know baby. I just don't know." If you knew Kristy then I want to ask you, "How did her life affect you?" Then

I want to ask you, "How did her death affect you?" You can see her again. I can hardly wait.

I sometimes ask God to give Kristy and Dani a message for me. I will say something like, "God, please tell them how much I miss them and that I long to see them again." I don't know if God relays that message to them or not but it does make me feel better. I do believe that He does things in ways that we cannot understand, so I don't count it out.

Then I think about what Kristy might say if she could look down and speak to us. I think it may be something like this:

My dear family and friends,

Oh, how I wish that you could just get a small glimpse of this glorious place that I now call home. I don't have the words to describe its beauty. Brother Paul was right when he said that even our imaginations could not come close to comprehending what heaven is like.

I was down by the river this morning. I was sitting on a bank letting the fresh cool water flow over my feet. Jesus came and sat down next to me. He put His arm around me and said, "Imagine, my child. Your life here hasn't even yet begun. You have all eternity ahead of you."

I then looked around and saw Dani running through a field of flowers with some other children. They were laughing and playing and having such a wonderful time. I don't think she has sat down since she's been here. She picks me beautiful flowers everyday.

I have met so many loved ones here who I did not know while living on earth. I talk with Ma Johnson and Grandma Southers everyday. The first time I saw them they knew exactly who I was. In fact, when I got here they brought Dani to me. When she saw me she came running as fast as her little legs could carry her.

It's so good seeing Grandma Palmer like I remembered her before she got sick. There is no sickness here. I don't have allergies to contend with anymore. There is no pain, fears, heartaches, disappointment, or sadness here.

I know that you miss me, but don't be sad for me. Our parting is not for long. Jesus is returning very soon, and we will be reunited again. I do hope you are ready to meet Him. Nothing is worth missing heaven for. I love you and hope to see you all again.

Love, Kristy

I thank you for reading "Grace I Never Knew." If you would be interested in having me share my testimony and the message of God's grace at your church, please contact me at terry.southers@yahoo.com. Our God is worthy to be praised!

Special Recognition

I would like to offer special recognition and thanks to the Grant Hospital Trauma Unit for all that they did. They are all such wonderful and gifted people. I can always rest assured that Kristy received the best care possible that last week of her life. I know that there was nothing more that the doctors and nurses of this fine hospital could have done to save her life. It was just God's will to bring Kristy home.

Lastly, but certainly not least, I want to recognize my son-in-law, Matt Woodcox, the father of my grandchildren. Since the loss of his wife and daughter, Matt has been through his share of trials and struggles as well. He, too, has experienced the remarkable grace of a loving God. Steph and I are proud of the way Matt has not allowed this tragedy to hinder his faith in God. We want Matt to know that we love and support him as he strives to move on with his new life.

Printed in the United States
202267BV00001B/157-1533/P